History of Japan

An Enthralling Journey Through Ancient Japanese Empires, the Shogunate Era, Cultural Renaissance, and Modern Period

© Copyright 2025 - All rights reserved.

The content contained within this book may not be reproduced, duplicated, or transmitted without direct written permission from the author or the publisher.

Under no circumstances will any blame or legal responsibility be held against the publisher, or author, for any damages, reparation, or monetary loss due to the information contained within this book, either directly or indirectly.

Legal Notice:

This book is copyright protected. It is only for personal use. You cannot amend, distribute, sell, use, quote, or paraphrase any part, or the content within this book, without the consent of the author or publisher.

Disclaimer Notice:

Please note the information contained within this document is for educational and entertainment purposes only. All effort has been executed to present accurate, up-to-date, reliable, and complete information. No warranties of any kind are declared or implied. Readers acknowledge that the author is not engaging in the rendering of legal, financial, medical, or professional advice. The content within this book has been derived from various sources. Please consult a licensed professional before attempting any techniques outlined in this book.

By reading this document, the reader agrees that under no circumstances is the author responsible for any losses, direct or indirect, that are incurred as a result of the use of the information contained within this document, including, but not limited to, errors, omissions, or inaccuracies.

Free limited time bonus

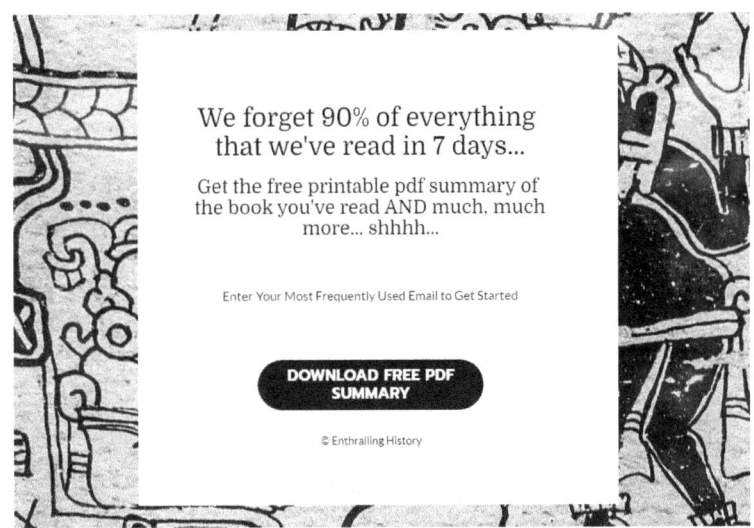

Stop for a moment. We have a free bonus set up for you. The problem is this: we forget 90% of everything that we read after 7 days. Crazy fact, right? Here's the solution: we've created a printable, 1-page pdf summary for this book that you're reading now. All you have to do to get your free pdf summary is to go to the following website:
https://livetolearn.lpages.co/enthrallinghistory/

Or, Scan the QR code!

Once you do, it will be intuitive. Enjoy, and thank you!

Table of Contents

INTRODUCTION 1
CHAPTER 1: EARLY JAPANESE KINGDOMS 3
CHAPTER 2: THE IMPERIAL GOLDEN AGE 12
CHAPTER 3: THE RISE OF THE SAMURAI 21
CHAPTER 4: THE KAMAKURA CONFLICT 32
CHAPTER 5: THE ASHIKAGA ERA 40
CHAPTER 6: THE SENGOKU PERIOD 52
CHAPTER 7: THE PEACEFUL EDO PERIOD 65
CHAPTER 8: THE MEIJI TRANSFORMATION 75
CHAPTER 9: THE SHŌWA ERA 83
CHAPTER 10: MODERN JAPAN 96
CONCLUSION 104
HERE'S ANOTHER BOOK BY ENTHRALLING HISTORY THAT YOU MIGHT LIKE 107
FREE LIMITED TIME BONUS 108
WORKS CITED 109
IMAGE SOURCES 111

Introduction

In 1944, anthropologist Ruth Benedict was given the task of explaining Japanese culture and society to an American audience. The two countries were locked in the Pacific theater of World War II. Because of this, Benedict could not travel to Japan. She was not an expert on Japan, but she was open-minded and determined to provide a well-balanced view. The result was a book, *The Chrysanthemum and the Sword*, which many still hail as a work of brilliance in comparative cultural studies. As Benedict explained, it was incredibly difficult for the Western mind to grasp the Japanese worldview. One way is to study the complicated history of this archipelago.

A short anecdote from Benedict's book can serve as a starting point of sorts. During the war, there were Japanese broadcasts about a Japanese air force captain who returned from battle, counted the number of planes that had returned, and then filed his report with his commanding officer. As soon as he had turned in his report, he dropped dead at the headquarters. It was discovered that he had been killed by a bullet wound he had suffered during battle. His body was already ice-cold. It was not the hero-pilot who had filed his report but rather his spirit, which had lingered to finish his duties.

"To Americans, of course, this is an outrageous yarn, "Benedict explained. "But educated Japanese did not laugh at this broadcast."[i] For

---

[i] Benedict, Ruth. *The Chrysanthemum and the Sword: Patterns of Japanese Culture.* Houghton Mifflin, 2005.

the average Japanese, this exemplified the nature of the war, which the Americans failed to grasp. For them, it was about American materialism and capitalism against Japanese spiritualism.

Japan's entry into World War II was driven primarily by imperial ambitions, economic pressures, and strategic considerations, particularly the need to secure access to vital natural resources in Southeast Asia. Japanese propaganda framed the conflict as a civilizational struggle between Western materialism and Eastern spiritualism, which served to justify military expansion.

Some contemporary Westerners may only know Japan by anime, Hello Kitty, and Nintendo, but they miss the context of Japan's current form by ignoring the story of a nation that has conquered and been conquered, a place of endless beauty and brutal warfare. Japan has long defied the Western view that Europe and its colonies dominated world history. This book will help you begin to understand the complexities of Japanese history, from the first humans who called Japan home to the current concerns of the modern Japanese citizen.

Chapter 1: Early Japanese Kingdoms

Many, especially the Japanese people themselves, have wondered when their society began. When did some of the key components of Japanese culture get their start? Rice paddy farming, Shinto beliefs, and a society based on a clear hierarchical structure all seem to have begun around 300 or 400 BCE after the Yayoi people moved into the area. Previously, there had been the Jōmon culture of hunter-gatherers, which had been living on the Japanese islands since 14,000 BCE.

The accepted wisdom is that tens of thousands of years ago, when parts of Japan were still connected to the Asian mainland due to lower sea levels, early humans crossed into what would be the nation of Japan. These humans, like all other humans of the time, relied on hunting and foraging for subsistence. They lived in settlements, but there was something distinctive about these people: they made pottery.

The term "Jōmon" actually means corded pottery, which is the identifier for these unnamed and somewhat mysterious people. The story goes that the Jōmon were conquered and replaced by the Yayoi people, who also came from the mainland (China, Korea, or both). They brought rice farming and bronze tools with them. But this story has been questioned recently.

Accelerator mass spectrometry (AMS) dating completed in the past ten years has shown that the Yayoi people came to Japan in 900 BCE, five hundred years earlier than archaeologists previously thought. This means that the Yayoi and Jōmon people lived in Japan simultaneously.

The implication is that the Yayoi violently conquered their new neighbors at an unbelievable speed, but this is a problematic explanation.

Some Yayoi pottery shows a mix of Jōmon styles and techniques alongside new forms brought in by migrants, which suggests that the two groups interacted and blended. DNA taken from remains at Jōmon and Yayoi sites both showed similarities with modern Japanese. This means that the Jōmon certainly didn't die out since their genetics carried on into modern-day populations.

This upending of ideas that were well established created an uproar in Japan, where the past remains a large part of the present. Japan is one of the most well-excavated countries in the world, with thousands of active sites being worked on every year. The Japanese held that the beginning of the Yayoi was the beginning of Japan, so questioning the date and how it happened was hard for the public to accept.

The Jōmon were not part of that tradition. They had lived in Japan, and they had particularly sophisticated pottery for the period. Many Jōmon burials have been found with artifacts such as combs, lacquerware, and small figurines. They had large settlements, but some archaeologists think the Jōmon might have faced real food shortages in certain regions, especially away from the coast, where seasonal changes made it harder to get enough to eat. Others argue they had a pretty stable diet overall, but it probably depended a lot on where they lived and what they had access to. For the most part, they lacked agriculture and metal tools, which allowed the Yayoi population to expand across the archipelago. This population growth, conservative Japanese historians say, is what led to the creation of the Japanese state.

However, modern research indicates that the Yayoi did not conquer the Jōmon and displace them. Instead, small groups of newcomers from the mainland arrived in Japan with new technology, and the Jōmon grew to accept these changes. Over hundreds of years, the two groups were blended into one until a new culture, called the Yayoi, could be identified as being distinct from the previous Jōmon.

With this out of the way, we can say that Japanese history begins with the Jōmon period, which started in 14,000 BCE, at the earliest. It seems that the Jōmon began making pottery in about 13,000 to 11,000 BCE, though this is still uncertain, as the pottery itself cannot be dated—only organic remains near the pottery can be.

It is believed that the creation of pottery reflects a more sedentary lifestyle. This lifestyle change might have come from the end of the Pleistocene Epoch around 11,700 years ago. Large game went extinct on the islands, so the people had to rely more on foraging, especially nuts from deciduous trees. This led to a need to process and store food, which, in turn, led to the creation of pottery.

The Jōmon lived in pit houses and used stone tools to dig out their houses and to work the wood that they used to cover their homes. They began to live more sedentary lifestyles, but this does not mean they collectively abandoned nomadic practices. They had large living sites that consisted of ten houses or more, but they also might have only used them for part of the year. These people cultivated some plants, but these appear not to have made up a large portion of their diet. They grew a wide range of crops, such as buckwheat, bottle gourd, and hemp.

Jōmon pottery is of interest to prehistorians worldwide. The pottery is identifiable, but it changed over time and in different geographical regions. The debate continues as to whether the Jōmon people discovered or were introduced to pottery. The dates given to many finds in Japan appear earlier than those found in China, which leads some to question the accepted theory that the Jōmon learned pottery-making from Chinese migrants. The stylistic commonalities in the pottery in certain areas have led researchers to believe that the Jōmon lived in tribes or similar societal structures.

The Jōmon period is exceptionally long, so it is broken up into various phases, though these phases cannot be clearly defined and are sometimes specific to a certain region. At times, the Jōmon lived in substantial dwellings in large settlements, though over time, some of those populations seem to have declined and were replaced by smaller huts. The Jōmon built large wooden structures, possibly even multi-story ones, and engaged in limited cultivation. They built stone circles and wooden post structures. Some alignments in those monuments suggest they had a sense of seasonal change or solar movement—hints of what you might call a rudimentary calendar.

One of the most intriguing types of Jōmon artifacts that have been found is the lacquerware items. Today, lacquer is harvested from domesticated trees. Each tree produces only a small amount of raw lacquer per year—often much less than 0.1 liters. Lacquer trees in the wild produce even less, which suggests that the Jōmon cultivated lacquer trees for their needs. Given that the trees must mature for eight to ten years before they can be harvested, this hints at well-planned cultivation.

The Jōmon mixed the lacquer with the oil from the egoma (or shiso) plant. They used two types of material to color the lacquer red: hematite and cinnabar. Black coloring was likely obtained using iron compounds. Wooden vessels and textiles were lacquered, and their appearance is only found in relatively wet sites that preserved this material.

Jōmon hunters developed bows and created pit traps to catch wild boar. They domesticated dogs and were skilled fishermen. Despite all of their advances, Jōmon skeletal remains suggest that many people suffered high mortality and possibly nutritional stress. In the Late Jōmon period, small quantities of grain have been found in pottery, but it was not until the arrival of farming populations from the Korean Peninsula in the early 1st millennium BCE that the people of Japan began to engineer their environment for agriculture.

This marks the beginning of the Yayoi period, which lasted from about 300 BCE to 300 CE. Yayoi agriculture in the early phase included cereals, such as buckwheat and barley, particularly in southern Kyūshū, though wet-rice cultivation soon became more important. The more predictable yields of these crops helped farming spread rapidly. This, in turn, led to higher birth rates and longer life expectancy, fueling a population increase across the Japanese islands. Over time, rice paddies with irrigation systems replaced or supplemented earlier dry-field cultivation, thus offering a more dependable food base.

By year 0, the Yayoi population is sometimes speculated to have reached several hundred thousand, though estimates vary. Chinese sources used the name "Wa" (or "Wo") to refer broadly to the peoples of Japan, and they engaged in trade—likely via Korean outposts—with mainland China and Korea. Some Japanese goods, including rice, might have been exchanged, and Chinese and Korean products likewise entered the archipelago. During the middle and late Yayoi period, rice increasingly became the dominant crop in many regions.

At the Yayoi site of Itazuke in Fukuoka Prefecture, evidence such as rice field remains, storage pits, dog bones, and deer or boar bones suggests a typical village economy. Children's jar burials have been found, sometimes in large ceramic jars apparently used just for that purpose. Near those burial sites, Chinese and Korean artifacts are often discovered in notable abundance.

Yayoi-era paddy systems included engineered features like sluice gates, irrigation canals, wells, and storage infrastructure. Competition over arable land appears in the archaeological record, and some sites show bronze and iron weaponry production and signs of armed conflict. The Chinese maintained interest in Yayoi (Wa) polities across the sea.

The Chinese paid particular attention to the first historically attested ruler in Japanese history, the shaman-queen Himiko, who lived from about 170 CE to 247 or 248 CE. At that time, the Japanese had not begun recording their history, so it is only through Chinese and Korean writers or archaeological evidence that we know anything about Himiko and her kingdom, Yamatai. This kingdom was composed of many smaller polities. The exact location of Yamatai is still debated, but it is believed to have been either in northern Kyūshū or central Honshu.

The Chinese noted that Himiko's rule was unusual in that she was a woman, but there is no indication that this was strange to the Yayoi people of the time. Still, Chinese leaders recognized her, giving her special status. The Chinese texts explain that after seventy or eighty years of disturbances and warfare among the various chieftains in the land of Wa, the Yayoi selected Himiko as their ruler, possibly because she was a woman since the period of conflict had been under the rule of a man. However, some female burials from the Yayoi period suggest that women held high status and might have acted as leaders.

What makes Himiko remarkable is her apparent control over a large part of Japan. It was said she held authority over as many as thirty separate polities. Also, she is important because she was the first Japanese leader in the historical record due to her interactions with the Chinese. Himiko was recognized as a "ruler friendly to Wei" by the state of Cao Wei during the Three Kingdoms period in Chinese history. Emissaries from Yamatai traveled to Emperor Cao Rui of Wei in 238 CE, apparently bearing gifts of slaves and cloth. While the Chinese authors put special emphasis on Himiko's magical abilities, Japan's early history includes rulers, male and female, who were believed to have spiritual powers and to communicate with the gods. For instance, Emperor Jinmu is traditionally seen as a descendant of the sun goddess Amaterasu and is said to have established the Japanese imperial line in 660 BCE. Though considered a legendary figure, his story reflects the early belief that political authority was rooted in divine ancestry.

In the Wei records, called the *Wei zhi*, the Chinese chroniclers give a description of Queen Himiko's burial, which gives us a look into the religious beliefs of the early Japanese. Priests conducted divination by burning bones and studying the cracks made by the fire for clues about the future. It was a practice the Chinese had seen before. Priests in the Shang dynasty (1600-1046 BCE) had similar methods of seeing into the future. This has led some to suggest that this, like bronze and agricultural techniques, might have reached Japan through cultural transmission from East Asia.

The Yayoi buried their dead in wooden coffins as well as large jars. They observed a period of mourning for more than ten days and then purified themselves through immersion in water, something that was later adopted into Shinto practices. The Yayoi beliefs are just the beginnings of what would become the indigenous religion of Japan.

Himiko was buried under a large mound, and one hundred attendants were buried with her to assist her in the afterlife. She was replaced by a relative named Iyo, who is said in later sources to have been thirteen years old.

At the time of her death, which is believed to have been in the 3rd century CE, Japan was entering into a new historical period that was noted for increased militarization and a shift toward more male-dominated leadership. It is called the Yamato period.

This period is often split into two. First came the Kofun period (250-538 CE), and the Asuka period followed (538-710 CE). The name "Kofun" comes from the Japanese word *kofun*, which is the type of burial mound distinctive to the period. Himiko's burial might have been among the earliest of these. They were often either square or circular mounds over burial chambers. Later examples have the famous keyhole shape with a round side and a more square side, sometimes surrounded by a moat.

The beginning of the Kofun period is marked by a great struggle between chiefdoms over local dominance. This led to a large increase in fortified structures and production, as well as the improvement of weapon technology. The Japanese became so skilled at war that they might have provided soldiers to aid both the Baekje (or Paekche) and Silla Kingdoms of Korea in the late 4th and early 5th centuries.

In the latter half of the 3rd century, there is some evidence to suggest the development of a particular confederation of states and clans around a central leader. This leader or king was associated with the Yamato lineage, and their rise to power is rooted in mystery. By the time the

Yamato kingship came to control much of Japan, they had developed a family history that included legendary characters who lived incredibly long lives and enjoyed relationships with the gods.

The Yamato confederation was centered around the area that is today the Nara Prefecture. At that time, the Yamato kings had to bring the various clans, which were powerful families, under their control. The clans were led by a patriarch who performed the necessary rituals to the clan's kami or spirit to ensure success. The members of these clans would become the nobility of the Yamato court, with the head of the Yamato line being the leader of them all.

The kings were called the "Great Kings of Yamato," and they were the precursors to the *tennō*, or emperors. The *Nihon Shoki* or *Chronicles of Japan*, which was written in the 700s, tried to trace the Yamato lineage back to 660 BCE. However, it leaves out rulers such as Himiko. One of the earliest Yamato kings with possible historical support was Yūryaku, who ruled in the 5th century CE and is believed to have been referred to as "Wakatakeru" in contemporary inscriptions. He is believed to have sent a letter to the Chinese emperor saying that he had conquered fifty-five countries of hairy men to the east and sixty-five barbarian countries to the west. Also, he and his armies crossed the sea to Korea and conquered ninety-five more countries.

It is impossible to say if this letter was in any way accurate, but the inscription of a sword from the period states, "When the court of the Great King Wakatakeru was in Shiki, I aided him in ruling the realm, and had this hundred-time-wrought sword made to record the history of my service."[i]

The first widely accepted Great King was Emperor Kinmei. His reign lasted from 539 to 571 CE. He gained the throne after his brother, Emperor Senka, died at seventy-three. His reign coincided with when it is believed Buddhism was first introduced to the islands and also the beginning of the Asuka period, when the center of Yamato power moved to the Asuka region, sixteen miles south of the modern-day city of Nara.

The Yamato clan's power grew greatly in this period. They ruled largely uncontested from the capital in Asuka. In 552, it is recorded that the king of Baekje sent a bronze statue of the Buddha to Emperor

---

[i] Walker, Brett L. *A Concise History of Japan.* Cambridge University Press, 2015.

Kinmei, along with artisans and monks. The introduction of Buddhism into the Yamato court led to a deep rift between the Mononobe clan, who wanted to continue to worship Japan's traditional deities (a practice now known as Shinto), and the Soga clan, who supported the adoption of Buddhism as the national religion.

Shinto had no founder or overarching doctrine. It centers around the kami, which can be gods, principles, supreme beings, or even the mind. One of the most well-known kami is Amaterasu, the goddess of the sun and the universe. According to legend, Amaterasu gave her grandson five rice grains from heaven and sent him to lead the people of Japan, becoming the first legendary emperor of the Yamato line.

The first written records of Shinto beliefs come from the *Kojiki* or *Records of Ancient Matters* from 712 CE and the previously mentioned *Nihon Shoki*. The *Kojiki* gives hundreds of classifications of kami with different functions. Today, the Shinto religion recognizes over four million kami.

At the time, Shinto was not a formal religion but rather a collection of clan-based rituals centered on the worship of kami. Each clan maintained its own rituals to honor the kami. In contrast, Buddhism arrived as a fully developed belief system with texts, ethics, and a sophisticated material culture. For the Soga clan, supporting Buddhism offered not only spiritual appeal but also a means to align with the political and cultural prestige of continental powers like China and Korea. The Mononobe clan viewed Buddhism as a foreign intrusion that threatened Japan's traditional spiritual foundations.

Summary Timeline — Early Japanese Kingdoms
- 14,000 BCE - Earliest Jōmon settlements established; people create cord-marked pottery, pit houses, and stone tools.
- 13,000–11,000 BCE - Development of pottery linked to a more settled, foraging lifestyle after the end of the Pleistocene.
- 900 BCE - Yayoi migrants arrive from the mainland, introducing rice cultivation, bronze tools, and ironworking.
- 300 BCE - 300 CE - Yayoi period flourishes; rice-paddy agriculture spreads, and population increases.
- 170 - 248 CE - Reign of Queen Himiko, first recorded ruler of Japan, who governs the kingdom of Yamatai and communicates with the Chinese Wei dynasty.

- 250 – 538 CE – Kofun period begins; large keyhole tombs built for rulers and nobles.
- 539 – 571 CE – Reign of Emperor Kinmei; introduction of Buddhism from the Korean Kingdom of Baekje starts the Asuka period and divides Japan's leading clans.

Chapter 2: The Imperial Golden Age

When the bronze Buddha statue came to Emperor Kinmei from Korea in 552, a plague struck Japan. Out of fear that this happened because of offense given to the kami, and on the advice of the Nakatomi and Mononobe clans, the statue was thrown into a canal. But then, the great hall of the imperial palace suddenly caught fire. Caught between two possibly vengeful gods, Emperor Kinmei did not take definitive action to resolve the dilemma.

Soga no Iname, the leader of the Soga clan, married his daughter, Soga no Kitashihime, to Emperor Kinmei. Together, they had eight children, including the future Emperor Yōmei and Princess Nukatabe, who became the chief wife of Emperor Bidatsu, the ruler after Kinmei. After Bidatsu and Yōmei died, there was a power struggle between the Mononobe and Soga clans. The Soga prevailed and installed Emperor Sushun, but the new ruler disliked being controlled by the head of the Soga clan, Soga no Umako, so Umako had the king assassinated in 592.

Princess Nukatabe, Umako's niece, was selected to sit on the Chrysanthemum Throne (the imperial throne), though these early rulers would not have been called emperors during their reign. However, they were posthumously given imperial titles, so these "Great Kings" are often called emperors in modern histories.

Princess Nukatabe was given the title and name of Empress Suiko. While the son of Emperor Yōmei, Prince Shōtoku, became regent and

Soga no Umako wielded considerable power, there is clear evidence that Suiko had a certain level of independence. During her reign, the Japanese government was modernized, and the Seventeen-Article Constitution was created in 604. This constitution was mainly notable for the heavy influence of Buddhist and Confucian ideology it promoted. Suiko was the first openly Buddhist monarch of Japan, and she promoted Buddhism throughout the land.

Suiko died in 628 after being on the throne for thirty-five years. She was succeeded by Emperor Jomei (593–641), grandson of Emperor Bidatsu. The head, or *ōmi*, of the Soga clan, Soga no Emishi, helped to install Jomei on the throne and held sway over the court. After Jomei's death, he was succeeded by his wife, Empress Kōgyoku. She ruled for less than four years and then abdicated to her brother, Emperor Kōtoku, who ruled until 654. Kōgyoku returned to the throne, though she was then known as Empress Saimei. She ruled until her death in 661.

She was followed by her son with Jomei, Emperor Tenji, who had been instrumental in overturning the Soga clan's control of the imperial court. The downfall of the powerful Soga clan came in 645 during an event known as the Isshi Incident. The Soga had long held dominance over court affairs, controlling key appointments and shaping imperial succession. However, their growing power alarmed Prince Naka no Ōe, the future Emperor Tenji, and his close ally, Nakatomi no Kamatari. Together, they orchestrated a dramatic coup during a court ceremony. With swords hidden beneath their robes, they launched a surprise attack on Soga no Iruka, the head of the clan, killing him in front of assembled courtiers. Shortly after, Iruka's father, Soga no Emishi, committed suicide, effectively ending the political power of the Soga. This violent turning point cleared the way for the Taika Reforms, a series of centralizing policies aimed at weakening clan autonomy and strengthening imperial rule. As a reward for his role in the coup, Kamatari was later granted the surname Fujiwara by Emperor Tenji in 669, founding one of the most influential families in Japanese history.

Tenji compiled the first legal code, the Ōmi Code, in Japanese history. This was a *ritsuryō*, which was a code based on Confucian ethics (focused on hierarchy and proper conduct) and Chinese Legalism (which emphasized strict laws and punishments). It served as both a criminal and administrative code.

Tenji died in 672 and was succeeded by his son, Emperor Kōbun, who only ruled for a few months. He was the son of an emperor, but his mother was of lower origins. In an event known as the Jinshin War, his army was defeated by his uncle's army. The war began as a struggle over succession after Emperor Tenji's death. He had favored Kōbun, though he had earlier considered naming his brother as heir. Kōbun's uncle, Prince Ōama, quietly gathered support and then led a successful military campaign against Kōbun. After his defeat, Kōbun committed suicide. His uncle became Emperor Tenmu. Tenmu was the first monarch to receive the title of *tennō*, or emperor, in his lifetime.

Then came the reigns of Empress Jitō and her grandson, Emperor Monmu. Empress Genmei came to the throne in 707. During her reign, the capital was moved to Nara, thus beginning the Nara period. The ancestry of the Yamato imperial line was officially codified in the *Kojiki* and *Nihon Shoki*, specifically that the imperial family descended from the sun goddess Amaterasu. The kingdoms under Yamato control during the Nara period were primarily in central Japan.

One critical part of the Nara period was the conquest of the Emishi people in the northeastern part of the archipelago. The Emishi were a hunter-gatherer group far removed from the Chinese influence that permeated the Nara court. They were in many ways a holdover from the Jōmon era. "Emishi" is a term used by Nara officials to describe these northern peoples. It possibly meant something like "hairy people" or "eastern barbarians."

Despite the Yamato depiction of total control over Japan, the northern regions differed greatly from the culture at the capital. The Satsumon and Okhotsk people on the island of Hokkaido and the peoples of Sakhalin and the Amur River Estuary had long remained outside the reach of Chinese, Buddhist, and Confucian influences. They were not part of the ritsuryō (penal and administrative) codes that defined life in the core provinces.

During the Nara period (710-784), the Yamato court launched repeated military campaigns against the Emishi as part of an ongoing effort to expand imperial control over the northeastern frontier. Fort Taga (near Sendai) was constructed in 724, and its commander held the title of chinjufu shogun, or commander of the defense of the north. The Emishi fighters continually destroyed Yamato forts and resisted the conquest. It was not until the Heian period (794-1185) that a general named Sakanoue no Tamuramaro (758-811) was appointed as chinjufu shogun, and the Emishi were finally and violently subjugated.

This conflict marked the culmination of the Yamato family's ascendancy to power. While they still faced rivals, it was only in political struggles within the ritsuryō framework. An elaborate court had evolved in the capital of Nara at the beginning of the Emishi wars. Buddhism became the official religion of the court, though Shinto was still practiced by the majority of the people. Imperial rituals also continued to be conducted according to Shinto traditions. In fact, after the death of a monarch, it was normal to move the capital as an act of purification. This practice ended when the capital remained at Nara through many emperors.

Genmei abdicated the Chrysanthemum Throne in preference to her daughter, Empress Genshō, who acted as regent to her nephew, Prince Obito. During Genshō's reign, the powerful courtier Fujiwara no Fuhito of the Fujiwara clan died. He had been instrumental in establishing the ritsuryō system by helping to create the Taihō Code and later the revised Yōrō Code, which organized Japan's government into a centralized bureaucracy, outlined civil and criminal laws, and defined the roles of officials, land distribution, and taxation. After he died in 720, he was given the posthumous title of Daijō-daijin, or "Chancellor of the Realm," the highest office in the imperial court.

The Fujiwara clan, which descended from the Nakatomi clan, had risen to power after helping to topple the great Soga clan. The honorary title of Fujiwara was given to Nakatomi no Kamatari by Emperor Tenji in 669, and the clan name was passed to his son, Fujiwara no Fuhito.

After Fuhito's death, Prince Nagaya (cousin to Empress Genshō) seized political control of the court. This set up a struggle between Nagaya and Fuhito's four sons: Muchimaro, Fusasaki, Maro, and Umakai. The four sons were able to bring Nagaya up on false charges, and he was sentenced to death. Prince Nagaya was forced to commit suicide, and his wife and children were killed at the same time. It is believed that Nagaya placed a curse on his enemies because the four sons of Fuhito died one after another during a smallpox outbreak in 737.

In 724, Prince Obito ascended to the throne as Emperor Shōmu, son of Emperor Monmu and grandson of Fujiwara no Fuhito. It was during Shōmu's reign that the deadly smallpox outbreak of 735-737 broke out. It killed an estimated 35 percent of Japan's population.

Shōmu was a devout Buddhist and attempted to establish official temples and nunneries in each province. He commissioned the building of a sixteen-meter-tall Buddha statue in Nara. He moved the capital temporarily to three different places over five years, but he eventually returned it to Nara. He abdicated the throne in 749 and became a Buddhist monk. His daughter, Empress Kōken, succeeded him.

The court was largely under the control of Fujiwara no Nakamaro during her reign, and she was replaced on the throne by her relative, Emperor Junnin, in 758. Nakamaro became Junnin's prime minister (*taishi*), but he was at odds with the retired Empress Kōken and her healer and advisor, the Buddhist priest Dōkyō. It was reported that Kōken and Dōkyō were also lovers. Emperor Junnin tried to remonstrate with Kōken on this account, but it only made her angry, and she ended up giving Dōkyō even more power within her court.

Nakamaro was supported by Emperor Shōmu and his consort Empress Kōmyō, but by 760, both of them had died. He also faced epidemics and economic issues connected to the cost of building a new palace and organizing a planned invasion of Korea. Kōken took the opportunity to become more involved in politics and challenged Nakamaro's supremacy. Suspecting that Kōken was planning to usurp his power in the court, Nakamaro began placing his sons in key offices. Kōken responded by promoting her own people. In 764, things took a turn when Nakamaro took the imperial seals and station bells from Emperor Junnin and left the capital for Ōmi Province.

Nakamaro's forces met those of the empress, and the Fujiwara were defeated. Nakamaro was executed. Empress Kōken came back to the throne as Empress Shōtoku. She continued to promote the priest, Dōkyō, higher in the court. It was believed the empress was going to make him emperor, but she died in 770. Dōkyō, without her support and facing the still powerful Fujiwara clan, was stripped of his titles and sent into exile.

The new monarch was Emperor Kōnin, Kōken's half-brother. It was said that the empress had left a letter naming him as her heir when she died. He reigned for eleven somewhat uneventful years and abdicated in favor of his son, Emperor Kanmu.

During Kanmu's reign, the scope of the emperor's powers reached its highest point. His reign lasted from 781 to 806, and he proved to be an active monarch. In 784, he moved the capital from Nara to Nagaoka-kyō. The capital would move again in 794 to Heian-kyō (Kyoto), which lends its name to the Heian period that began in the same year.

Kanmu also appointed two of the earliest generals to hold the title Sei-i Taishogun, or "Barbarian-subduing General": Ōtomo no Otomaro and Sakanoue no Tamuramaro. While the title would later become synonymous with the shogunate, at this time, it referred to a military commander tasked with subduing the Emishi in northern Honshu. Tamuramaro is remembered best for subduing the Emishi and is a celebrated military figure in Japanese legend. He went on to become war minister after Kanmu died in 806.

Heian-kyō became the center of a rich court where several different Buddhist sects flourished, despite lingering suspicion after Dōkyō's fall. Courtiers exchanged poems celebrating the fragility of life, best exemplified in the waka poems. Men in the court still wrote poems in Chinese, but courtly women wrote in newly developed Japanese scripts, giving their poems a heightened significance to later audiences. The nobles of Heian enjoyed music, appreciated the scent of incense, and dressed according to the seasons. The emperor was at the center of it all, and aristocrats often commented on his shining presence, like a god amongst mortals.

Far-reaching trade networks spread out from the capital following canals, rivers, and roads. These networks reached the far corners of the empire, and trade was monitored by government officials in the great marketplaces of Heian and the western capital, Dazaifu. Coinage was typically done in copper, and the royal privilege to mint coins was a rare and lucrative gift. Traders also bartered items since coin circulation was limited. A wise buyer knew that while the markets in the capital had a wider selection, the prices were better in smaller markets in the countryside.

The average peasant worked the land and was a foreign figure to those inside the imperial court. Noble men and women often complained of having to go to temples alongside ordinary citizens who did not dress or behave in what they considered an appropriate fashion. Worst of all to a noble's senses was the presence of beggars who regularly visited Buddhist temples and Shinto shrines.

Any important activity was postponed until the proper divinations could be performed. Signs were studied to determine if a particular military campaign, wedding, or festival would be a success. The Chinese zodiac was consulted, along with interpretations of Chinese cosmology. The calendar was based on the lunar cycle, and everything required a balance between the forces of yin and yang. The substances of the universe were wood, fire, earth, metal, and water. In an increasingly patriarchal society, male children were highly valued, while a woman's inability to give birth to a male heir might be grounds for divorce.

Kanmu was succeeded first by his son, Emperor Heizei, and then by his second son, Emperor Saga. Heizei abdicated after less than three years due to illness, but when Saga fell ill, Heizei mounted an unsuccessful rebellion against his brother that was put down by Sakanoue no Tamuramaro.

The Fujiwara continued their dominance in the imperial court. Saga was not only the son of a Fujiwara princess, but his top officials were almost all from the Fujiwara clan. After Saga abdicated, the throne passed to another of Kanmu's sons, Emperor Junna. This period saw the rise of Fujiwara no Yoshifusa.

Junna abdicated in 833, and the crown passed to Emperor Ninmyō, son of Emperor Saga. Initially, Ninmyō selected Prince Tsunesada, a son of Junna, to be the heir, but Yoshifusa was opposed to the idea, favoring his nephew and the son of Ninmyō, Prince Michiyasu. The emperor was eventually convinced, and a struggle ensued, with Yoshifusa coming out victorious and Michiyasu becoming Emperor Montoku.

Yoshifusa remained in control and then became the regent (*sesshō*) under Emperor Seiwa, Montoku's son. As regent, Yoshifusa governed the country completely. He died in 872, but his example of boy-emperors with Fujiwara regents was followed for several years.

Yoshifusa's adopted son, Fujiwara no Mototsune, became regent of the next four emperors. He invented the **position** of kampaku regent, which was essentially a regent for an adult emperor. The Fujiwara became the de facto rulers of Japan in the 10th and 11th centuries, effectively ruling through puppet emperors. They reached their peak under a descendant of Mototsune, Fujiwara no Michinaga (966-1028), who was the father of six empresses or royal consorts and the grandfather of three emperors. He is widely believed to have inspired the Genji character in the famous Japanese novel, *The Tale of Genji*, which was written when Michinaga was in power. *The Tale of Genji* is a classic work of literature recognized throughout the world as one of the first novels and the first written by a woman.

With the ascendancy of Emperor Go-Sanjō (1068-1073), the Fujiwara clan's power began to decline. Many members of the Minamoto clan took their place, but the power of the military also increased at this time. A new class, the *bushi* (samurai) or warriors, grew in power.

Summary Timeline – The Imperial Golden Age

- 552 CE – King of Baekje sends a bronze Buddha statue to Emperor Kinmei, introducing Buddhism to Japan.
- 592 CE – Assassination of Emperor Sushun; Princess Nukatabe becomes Empress Suiko.
- 604 CE – Seventeen-Article Constitution created under Empress Suiko and Prince Shōtoku, blending Buddhist and Confucian ideals.
- 628 CE – Death of Empress Suiko after thirty-five years on the throne.
- 645 CE – Isshi Incident: Prince Naka no Ōe and Nakatomi no Kamatari overthrow the Soga clan; Taika Reforms begin.
- 669 CE – Emperor Tenji grants Kamatari the surname Fujiwara, founding the Fujiwara clan.
- 672 CE – Jinshin War between Emperor Kōbun and Prince Ōama; victory of Ōama, who becomes Emperor Tenmu.
- 707 CE – Empress Genmei ascends the throne; capital moved to Nara, beginning the Nara period.
- 720 CE – Death of Fujiwara no Fuhito; posthumously named Chancellor of the Realm.
- 724 CE – Emperor Shōmu begins his reign; smallpox epidemic strikes Japan in 735-737.
- 749 CE – Shōmu abdicates and becomes a monk; succeeded by Empress Kōken.
- 764 CE – Fujiwara no Nakamaro's rebellion; Empress Kōken returns to the throne as Empress Shōtoku.

- 770 CE – Death of Empress Shōtoku; Emperor Kōnin succeeds her.
- 781 CE – Emperor Kanmu begins reign; moves capital to Nagaoka-kyō (784) and then to Heian-kyō (Kyoto) in 794.
- 806 CE – Death of Emperor Kanmu; beginning of the Heian period.
- 872 CE – Death of Fujiwara no Yoshifusa, first regent (*sesshō*) to rule for a child emperor.
- 1028 CE – Death of Fujiwara no Michinaga, the peak of Fujiwara dominance.
- 1068–1073 CE – Reign of Emperor Go-Sanjō; Fujiwara power declines; rise of the warrior class.

Chapter 3: The Rise of the Samurai

The beginnings of the warrior class that would come to rule Japan can be traced back to the late 9th and early 10th centuries, especially during the campaigns against the Emishi in the north. These conflicts contributed to a slow decentralization of military authority. Men who made their living using weapons at this time were called *bushi*, a term often translated as "warrior." During the Heian period, many of the classic weapons and armor became established, such as the tachi or long sword, the naginata or glaive, and the distinctive ō-yoroi armor for cavalry and dō-maru for infantry.

Semi-independent nobles from Kyoto relied on these men-at-arms to provide protection and for peacekeeping duties in their provinces. A patron-client relationship developed between the bushi and local administrators, and it was in this way that warriors became part of the extended political network that radiated from the capital.

At the top of these military groups were often descendants of imperial or noble families, especially younger sons who had been removed from the line of succession. These descendants were given surnames to denote their clans or houses. Over time, these groups came to represent military powers that could be called on by emperors or retired emperors for support. These private armies were used throughout the Heian period to put down rebellions and challenge imperial authority.

Any high-ranking bushi who served the emperor, the imperial family, or the nobility could be referred to as a samurai, a word derived from *saburau*, meaning "to serve." An example of a Heian period **samurai** was Taira no Masakado, who was descended from Emperor Kanmu's great-grandson, Prince Takamochi. The prince had been demoted to commoner status and sent to the Kantō region, where he became a powerful landholder. Masakado is best remembered for leading a rebellion and declaring himself the "new emperor." His uprising failed, and he was killed, but his legend persisted. He eventually gained status as a vengeful spirit and even as a protective deity in some local cults.

Many members of the warrior class began to harbor political ambitions, which would lead to the eventual rise of the Heishi (members of the Taira clan) and Genji (members of the Minamoto clan). The Heishi were divided into several major lines named after the emperors from whom they were descended: Kanmu Heishi, Ninmyō Heishi, Montoku Heishi, and Kōkō Heishi. Taira no Kiyomori (1118-1181) was from the Kanmu Heishi line and took control of the Taira clan after his father's death in 1153. By that time, the two major rival samurai clans were the Taira and the Minamoto.

The rivalry between them erupted into open conflict during the Heiji rebellion of 1159-1160. Before the rebellion, power struggles at court had seen both clans acting in shifting alliances. Minamoto no **Yoshitomo** and Fujiwara no Nobuyori attempted to seize control of the government, briefly taking Emperor Nijō and the retired Emperor Go-Shirakawa into custody. However, Taira no Kiyomori swiftly countered their coup, defeating the Minamoto forces and executing their leaders. With this victory, Kiyomori rose to a dominant position in court politics, setting the stage for the Taira clan's brief supremacy in the late Heian period.

Minamoto no Yoshihira (with antlers on his helmet) in o-royoi armor during the Heiji rebellion.[1]

The leader of the Genji was Minamoto no Yoshitomo, and his chief ally was Fujiwara no Nobuyori, who was close to Emperor Go-Shirakawa. Some opposed the high rank of Nobuyori within the court, especially the influential Fujiwara no Michinori (also known as Shinzei). Shinzei was a chief advisor to Emperor Nijō and an ally of Taira no Kiyomori. Yoshitomo and Kiyomori had worked together to defeat the rebels in the Hōgen rebellion in 1156, which was a violent conflict among court factions over imperial succession and influence. These short but brutal court wars, known as disturbances (*ran* in Japanese), were driven by rivalries between noble houses and warrior clans seeking to control the throne through the use of military force. Yoshitomo and Kiyomori's paths had diverged after the Hōgen rebellion, and they now found themselves on opposite sides of the struggle between Nobuyori and Shinzei.

In 1159, Kiyomori left Kyoto for a time. Seeing this as an opportunity, Nobuyori and Yoshitomo attacked the Sanjō Palace, abducted the former Emperor Go-Shirakawa, and set the building on fire after killing many of the staff. They then attacked Shinzei, who escaped capture, only to be found and decapitated later.

Nijō was forced to name Nobuyori as imperial chancellor; however, his victory was short-lived. Kiyomori heard of the rebellion and returned to the capital in haste. Nobuyori and his Minamoto allies were not prepared to defend the city. Kiyomori made peace offerings to Nobuyori, but these were only to buy time. The former Emperor Go-Shirakawa and Emperor Nijō were able to escape and join Kiyomori's side. With imperial authority now backing him, the Taira leader was permitted to move against Nobuyori and his ally Yoshitomo in the imperial palace.

A fierce battle between the sons of Yoshitomo and Kiyomori, Yoshihira and Shigemori, respectively, took place. The Taira force initially retreated, and the Minamoto pursued, but this was part of the ploy by Kiyomori, who then sent a force to occupy the palace. The Minamoto, cut off and disorganized, were routed, and Taira no Kiyomori was victorious.

Yoshitomo attempted to flee but was betrayed and killed shortly after his defeat. Kiyomori showed compassion and spared the lives of some of Yoshitomo's younger sons, sending them into exile. These sons— Yoritomo, Noriyori, and Yoshitsune—would go on to play a role in the history of Japan.

The result of the Heiji rebellion was that the Taira under Kiyomori were now in control of the government, and imperial power had been weakened even further. The Minamoto and Taira were even more deeply divided, with extreme animosity between them. The rebellion spawned *The Tale of Heiji*, which exists in oral, visual, and written forms and is closely connected to *The Tale of Hōgen* that precedes it.

In the years that followed, Emperor Nijō remained on the throne, but his authority was hollow. The real power belonged to Kiyomori and the retired Emperor Go-Shirakawa. In 1165, Nijō abdicated in favor of his infant son and died shortly after at the age of twenty-two. His death marked another shift in power. Kiyomori continued to strengthen his position, rising to the rank of Daijō-daijin in 1167, the highest office in the imperial court. He moved the seat of government briefly to Fukuhara and arranged marriages that tied the Taira clan directly to the imperial line. Former Emperor Go-Shirakawa and others began to grow tired of the Taira's rule in the following years.

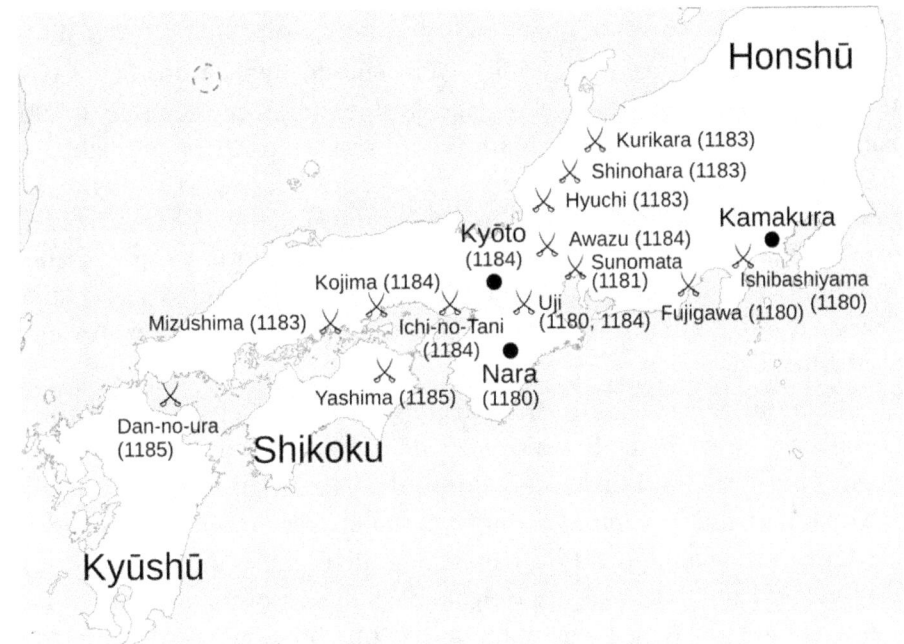

Battles of the Genpei War.[a]

In 1171, Taira no Kiyomori, the de facto ruler of Japan, arranged for the marriage of his daughter to Emperor Takakura. This couple had a son, Prince Tokihito, in 1178. Two years later, in 1180, Kiyomori staged a coup and forced his rivals to resign or be banished. He also imprisoned former Emperor Go-Shirakawa. Kiyomori then forced Takakura to abdicate, and Tokihito ascended the throne at just two years of age. This child emperor was later named Emperor Antoku.

Kiyomori's complete control caused many of his allies and provincial samurai to turn against him. Prince Mochihito, son of Emperor Go-Shirakawa, felt Kiyomori had gone too far and pushed his claim to the imperial throne. He called on the Minamoto to rise against the Taira and to overthrow Kiyomori. This is often cited as the beginning of what would be called the Genpei War, a civil war that once again pitted the Taira clan against the Minamoto clan in a struggle over control of Japan.

In mid-1180, Prince Mochihito sent out his call for aid. He was helped by Minamoto no Yorimasa, a poet and samurai who had once been friendly with Kiyomori but had turned against the Taira in favor of his clan. Yorimasa had become a monk upon retiring from the military, but he helped Mochihito gain support and agreed to lead the Minamoto forces.

In June of 1180, Mochihito and Yorimasa, with about 1,500 men, including Buddhist warrior monks, were chased by Taira forces across the Uji River near Byōdō-in, a Buddhist temple, and pulled up the planks of the bridge behind them. The Taira were led by an eighteen-year-old general named Tadatsuna, who became a legendary figure for his actions in the Battle of Uji. The Taira overcame the Minamoto army, and Yorimasa committed seppuku (ritual suicide) in the temple. Prince Mochihito was captured and killed shortly after the end of the battle. However, this did not end the Minamoto clan's desire for revenge against the Taira.

Minamoto no Yoritomo, the exiled son of the defeated and killed Yoshitomo, now made his move to defeat the hated Taira. He had grown up in exile and had married into the Hōjō clan. With the deaths of Mochihito and Yorimasa, Yoritomo established himself as the head of the Minamoto clan and set his capital at Kamakura in the Kantō region of Honshu. Kamakura was not only an ancient seat of the Minamoto but also a natural fortress, being surrounded on three sides by mountains and one side by the ocean.

In September 1180, Yoritomo met the Taira forces in the Battle of Ishibashiyama, where he was defeated but managed to escape. The Taira defeated other Minamoto forces later in the year but were unable to strike a definitive blow against the rebels. In the spring of 1181, Taira no Kiyomori died of a severe illness. It was said his fever was so high that those who touched him received burns on their hands.

The Taira forces now fell into the hands of Kiyomori's son, Munemori. A famine then raged through Japan, and the war was effectively put on hold for two years while the people coped with these harsh conditions. When hostilities resumed in the spring of 1183, it seemed that a great change had occurred to the fortunes of each side. The climax was perhaps the Battle of Kurikara Pass on June 2nd, 1183.

Taira no Koremori, the grandson of the late Kiyomori, organized an army to take revenge on Minamoto no Yoshinaka, who had previously invaded Taira land. Koremori divided his forces into two, with one going through the Kurikara Pass. Yoshinaka met his forces there and held an extremely formal battle with duels between samurai. This was simply a distraction to allow the other Minamoto forces to surround the Taira. They first let oxen with lit torches attached to their horns into the Taira lines and then ambushed them.

Yoshinaka wanted to defeat not only the Taira clan but also his cousin, Minamoto no Yoritomo, and gain control of the Minamoto clan. He kidnapped former Emperor Go-Shirakawa but was pursued by Yoritomo's brother, Yoshitsune, and was killed when he made a last stand at Awazu in Ōmi Province. The Minamoto, now united, turned their attention back to the Taira, who were gathering forces near the inland sea.

The Minamoto successfully defeated the Taira at Ichi-no-Tani in March of 1184. After a year of preparation, the main Taira army came under assault at the Battle of Yashima (Takamatsu). Yoshitsune tricked the Taira into thinking they were being attacked on land, so they fled in boats on the inland sea. Famously, a "pretty lady" with the Taira raised a fan and dared the Minamoto soldiers on the shore to shoot it from her hand. A soldier named Nasu no Yoichi rode into the water on horseback and did just that.

Many of the Taira were able to escape to Dan-no-ura, where a naval battle took place. This battle started in favor of the Taira, but with the changing of the tides, the Minamoto had the upper hand. This was the final defeat of the Taira clan and the end of the war.

Emperor Antoku and his grandmother, Taira no Tokiko (the widow of Kiyomori), are both said to have committed suicide by throwing themselves into the water. Many Taira commanders committed ritual suicide upon seeing that they were losing. Some of the imperial regalia were thrown into the sea but were said to have been found by divers.

The Taira dominance in the capital was over. The Minamoto took control, with Yoritomo as the clear leader. A new emperor had already been selected, the grandson of Go-Shirakawa, Emperor Go-Toba. The only person left to challenge Yoritomo's power was Emperor Go-Shirakawa and his half-brother and head general, Yoshitsune, who was made governor of Ōmi Province. Go-Shirakawa tried to give additional lands and titles to Yoshitsune, but Yoritomo nullified these appointments.

Yoshitsune was then given imperial authority to oppose Yoritomo, but Yoritomo discovered the plot. Yoshitsune was forced to flee Kyoto in 1185. He was able to find protection with the Fujiwara clan in Mutsu, but he was eventually betrayed. Yoshitsune committed seppuku when Yoritomo's forces found him. Go-Shirakawa and Yoritomo were reconciled after Yoshitsune's death.

In December of 1185, Go-Shirakawa granted Yoritomo the power to collect taxes and name constables of provinces. In 1192, Go-Shirakawa died at the age of sixty-six, and Yoritomo was granted the title Sei-i Taishogun or "commander in chief of expeditionary forces against the barbarians," typically called simply shogun. This is often considered the beginning of the shogunate period. While Go-Toba remained the emperor, his role was largely ceremonial. While Kyoto remained the official capital, the home of Yoritomo in Kamakura was where the real power resided.

As shogun, Yoritomo was ostensibly the leader of all samurai. This would mark the beginning of what is considered the feudal period in Japan. Yoritomo's shogunate did not last long, for he died in 1199. The role of shogun was considered hereditary, so Yoritomo's son, Minamoto no Yoriie, became shogun when he was only seventeen years old. He was controlled largely by his mother's father, Hōjō Tokimasa of the Hōjō clan. After a short reign, he was forced to abdicate and was succeeded by his brother, Minamoto no Sanetomo.

Sanetomo was nothing more than a puppet used by his mother, Hōjō Masako, in her power struggles with her father, Tokimasa. Sanetomo lived in constant fear of assassination and chose to pursue a career in the relatively powerless imperial court. He also focused on his poetry, becoming a well-regarded waka poet. However, he was eventually assassinated by his nephew in 1219. The assassin was executed, which ended their line of the Minamoto clan.

The shogun then became, like the emperors in previous generations, a puppet controlled by a *shikken* (regent) from the Hōjō clan. This clan, which had previously held little power and is believed to have descended from the Taira clan in Izu Province, now effectively ruled the country from Kamakura. They faced no real opposition until 1221, when former Emperor Go-Toba led a revolt against the shogunate. However, the Hōjō and their samurai soundly defeated him.

The third regent, Hōjō Yasutoki, created the Council of State, or Hyōjōshū, in 1225 and then created the Goseibai Shikimoku in 1232, which established the first true code of laws of the Kamakura shogunate. It steered the country away from the Chinese-style Confucian codes of the past and into a more militaristic legal framework. This code remained in effect in some form for the next 635 years.

At the same time, a growing menace was in the process of conquering portions of Korea. Between 1231 and 1270, the Mongol Empire conquered the Kingdom of Goryeo on the Korean Peninsula. The Mongols then set their sights on the Japanese archipelago just across the strait. In 1260, Kublai Khan was declared khagan and ruler of the vast Mongol Empire. Six years later, the Mongols and Koreans sent emissaries to Japan. They did this on six different occasions.

All of these attempts at communication were rebuffed. In 1274, it was decided that a Mongolian and Korean force would invade Japan. The invading force was about thirty thousand strong, with Japan only able to provide about six thousand warriors. These defenders were organized under the leadership of the Hōjō regency, with Hōjō Tokimune acting as the de facto commander in chief. Guided by the Zen monk Mugaku Sogen, Tokimune turned inward through meditation to confront his fear of the invasion. This spiritual resolve inspired him to promote Zen Buddhism throughout Japan.

The Mongolian forces first landed on Tsushima Island and quickly conquered it. They moved on to Iki Island, which they also took. Then, they landed at Hakata Bay on Kyūshū Island, which was the site of the Battle of Bun'ei. A large portion of the Mongolian fleet was lost due to storms, and the few who managed to land faced fierce resistance.

Still, the actual fighting was brief and uncoordinated. The Mongolian generals withdrew rather than pursue the Japanese further into unknown terrain at night. The invasion was abandoned, and the Mongolian and Korean forces that survived returned to the mainland.

To the Japanese, it seemed the invaders had disappeared overnight. But they were certain another invasion was on the horizon. The samurai trained more, and fortifications were constructed around the islands. In 1275, Kublai Khan sent another group of emissaries who refused to leave until the Japanese provided a reply. Tokimune responded by having the emissaries beheaded. Their bodies were sent back to China. The inevitable second invasion came in 1281.

This time, the Mongolian Yuan dynasty was able to provide a large force of possibly 140,000 soldiers (though this number might be exaggerated). These men were separated into two massive fleets. The first and smaller fleet advanced ahead of schedule, taking Tsushima and Iki but failing to land a sizable force at Hakata Bay due to the new Japanese fortifications, including a defensive wall. They were forced to take the islands of Shika and Noko instead. The Japanese counterattacked and were able to destroy a few ships.

The second fleet eventually arrived, and the two fleets again attacked Hakata Bay. Despite being able to land troops, the invasion reached a stalemate. Then, in August, a great typhoon, which the Japanese called the "Divine Wind" or kamikaze, struck the islands. This storm, along with the one that helped end the 1274 invasion, came to be seen as a supernatural force of protection.

A large number of ships were destroyed, and Yuan soldiers were left stranded in the sea or on some of the islands. The surviving ships abandoned the remaining soldiers and returned to China. The Japanese killed most of the Mongolian, Korean, and northern Chinese soldiers they found. However, they often spared southern Chinese conscripts, believing they had been forced into the invasion, though many were still enslaved.

While the Japanese victories were significant, Japan did not acquire any new lands, so the shogunate could not properly reward the samurai who had fought against the Yuan. This undermined the power of the Hōjō and their control of the shogunate. It also led to an increase in Japanese pirates who raided the Korean and Chinese coasts.

The loss to the Yuan was critical, as their naval power had been devastated. Korea's ability to supply ships was also crippled, having exhausted its natural resources in building the fleets. Chinese officials increasingly saw an invasion of Japan as futile, convinced that the Japanese were both brave and warlike.

Summary Timeline — The Rise of the Samurai

- 1153 CE - Death of Taira no Tadamori; his son, Taira no Kiyomori, assumes leadership of the Taira clan.
- 1156 CE - Hōgen Rebellion: conflict over imperial succession; Taira and Minamoto clans rise to prominence.
- 1159-1160 CE - Heiji Rebellion: Kiyomori defeats Minamoto no Yoshitomo and consolidates power.
- 1165 CE - Death of Emperor Nijō; Kiyomori gains further influence at court.
- 1167 CE - Kiyomori appointed Daijō-daijin (chancellor), the highest office in the imperial court.

- 1171 CE – Kiyomori's daughter marries Emperor Takakura, linking the Taira clan to the imperial line.
- 1178 CE – Birth of Prince Tokihito, later Emperor Antoku.
- 1180 CE – Kiyomori forces Emperor Takakura to abdicate; Antoku, age two, becomes emperor. Prince Mochihito and Minamoto no Yorimasa lead a rebellion, beginning the Genpei War.
- 1181 CE – Death of Taira no Kiyomori; famine strikes Japan.
- 1183 CE – Minamoto victory at Battle of Kurikara Pass, the turning point of the Genpei War.
- 1184 CE – Battle of Ichi-no-Tani; Taira forces defeated by Minamoto no Yoshitsune.
- 1185 CE – Naval Battle of Dan-no-ura; Taira clan destroyed, Emperor Antoku dies.
- 1192 CE – Minamoto no Yoritomo appointed shogun; Kamakura shogunate established.
- 1219 CE – Assassination of Shogun Minamoto no Sanetomo; end of the Minamoto line.
- 1221 CE – Emperor Go-Toba's failed rebellion; Hōjō clan solidifies power.
- 1225 CE – Hōjō Yasutoki establishes the Council of State (Hyōjōshū).
- 1232 CE – Goseibai Shikimoku code enacted; foundation of samurai law.
- 1260 CE – Kublai Khan becomes Mongol ruler.
- 1274 CE – First Mongol invasion repelled at Hakata Bay
- 1281 CE – Second Mongol invasion fails; end of Mongol threat.

Chapter 4: The Kamakura Conflict

The story of Buddhism began, perhaps, when Siddhartha Gautama found enlightenment in the yoga posture of dhyāna, which the West often translates as "meditation," though the meaning is much deeper than that word implies. Siddhartha went on to become the Buddha and the founder of Buddhism. Around a thousand years after the founding of Buddhism, a monk named Bodhidharma is said to have brought Buddhism to China in a form that would become known as Chan Buddhism. This was centered around the use of meditation to achieve self-awareness.

The character for Chan is pronounced "Zen" in Japan. Its focus was on meditation practices and finding one's own inner Buddha. Zen Buddhism does not worship any particular gods. While it emphasizes direct experience over scripture, it still draws from important sutras, such as the Heart Sutra and Diamond Sutra. Many famous Zen sayings have been passed down through the generations.

The Japanese monk Dōgen established the Sōtō Zen school in Japan in the 13th century after being taught in China. Dōgen was most likely born into the Minamoto clan around the year 1200. After his mother's death, he became a monk at a young age and became fixated on deeper philosophical questions. If humanity is born with the Buddha's nature, which many Buddhist sects teach, then why do holy people need to seek enlightenment? Dōgen was encouraged to find the answer by **studying** Chan Buddhism in China.

He made the journey in 1223 and eventually found a teacher, Rujing, who led him to realize the fundamentals of what would become Sōtō Zen Buddhism, which Dōgen would teach in Japan. The answer to Dōgen's question was essentially that to reveal one's natural enlightenment was to study oneself, and in order to do that, one must forget oneself. This seemingly contradictory concept is similar to many parts of Zen Buddhism that outsiders often fail to comprehend.

Dōgen returned to Japan and began to deliver the teachings of Zen Buddhism. His followers built the Eihei-ji Temple, which remains one of the two main centers for Sōtō Zen practice and study today.

Dōgen died in 1253. He is remembered best for bringing Zen Buddhism to Japan and for his focus on dhyāna (Japanese: *zazen*), which is often translated as seated meditation. This type of meditation was connected to *hishiryō*, or "non-thinking" or "beyond thinking," a state of mind that Westerners often struggle to define.

Mugaku Sogen (also known as Bukko) came to Japan from Song China and was welcomed as a Zen monk by the regent Hōjō Tokimune. Sogen advised Tokimune during the Mongol invasions. He was awarded a temple, Engaku-ji, in 1282, where he served as chief priest. He died in 1286.

While Zen began to gain footholds in the nobility and the samurai, it was not until the appearance of Keizan that Zen started to spread among the common people. Keizan founded the other great center of Sōtō Zen, the temple of Sōji-ji. Keizan also supported the training of women in Zen Buddhism. He died in 1325.

The infusion of Shinto and Zen beliefs into the moral code of the samurai (later called bushidō) under Tokimune elevated this warrior class, giving the samurai a dose of wisdom and serenity. Tokimune is said to have formally become a Zen monk near the end of his life in April 1284. He was succeeded by his son, Sadatoki, who continued to consolidate the power of the Hōjō and resigned as regent in 1301, though many claimed he continued to rule until he died in 1311.

In 1301, a new emperor was crowned, Go-Nijō. He was the ninety-fourth emperor of Japan, according to tradition. The shogun in that year was Prince Hisaaki, a member of the Minamoto clan. After Sadatoki's apparent retirement, he was succeeded by Hōjō Morotoki, who ruled as regent from 1301 until he died in 1311. He was succeeded by Takatoki, who was just eight years old when he became shikken in 1316.

During this time, another item closely associated with Japanese culture today was beginning to spread across the country: tea. Japan had grown and used tea for centuries, but it wasn't until the mid-13th and early 14th centuries that tea began to see widespread consumption. Kyoto and Kamakura, which under the Hōjō regency had grown into a city of seventy thousand inhabitants, became centers for the tea trade. The warrior class had newfound stability and wealth, and with that, they began to enjoy the finer things in life, including tea.

Much of what is known of tea production and consumption from the late 13th and into the 14th centuries comes from the writings of Sadaaki, the head of the lesser branch of the Hōjō clan called Kanazawa. Sadaaki's correspondence shows us that the cultivation of tea was primarily done by monks. The best tea was "early tea" picked in April. Tea could be purchased as loose whole leaves, compressed into bricks for storage and trade, or finely ground into powder—what we now know as matcha. Tea fields were small, usually less than 0.3 acres. There was also "mountain tea," which was cultivated sporadically in the countryside by common folk. This tea was typically of lesser quality and, therefore, less expensive.

A critical change in tea production occurred in the mid-13th century with the introduction of stone tea grinders from China. The use of these grinders resulted in a finer and sweeter tea. It, along with the development of shade-grown tea, gave Japanese tea its distinctive green color. This brought tea out of medicinal use and into a drink for enjoyment. Along with this came the tea whisk, which helped enhance the flavor, and the first methods for preserving tea leaves. Soon, tea was a party beverage and a popular gift.

Buddhist monks performed rituals that required certain tea, and elaborate games were held at parties in which participants guessed the best quality tea. However, the famous Japanese tea ceremony had yet to be perfected. Still, during the Kamakura shogunate, tea became a much more important part of everyday Japanese life, something that has lasted to the present day.

The Kanazawa might have been an offshoot of the main Hōjō line, but they were still powerful players in Kamakura. Tea flowed from the fields of the family temple of Shōmyōji into the capitals of Japan. The temple also had a stone tea grinder, so unground tea was often sent there to be processed. Sadaaki recorded numerous gifts of varying expense given to those he maintained as political allies, friends, family, and those with whom he hoped to ingratiate himself.

At Shōmyōji, Sadaaki also had a "Pure Land garden" or Jōdō garden, which was built by the gardener priest, Shōitsu. This garden included a shrine for the Amida Buddha and a pond with an island in the center connected via a bridge. Excavations of the site have indicated that the pond also featured a pebbled beach. Japanese gardens date back to the Heian period and were usually spots to attract kami or spirits. By the time of the Kamakura shogunate, gardens had become much more elaborate, and with the rise of Zen Buddhism, the first gardens devoted to meditation were designed. These gardens could be considered the precursor to the famous Japanese Zen gardens.

While the Kamakura period ushered in many quintessential Japanese traditions, with the regency of Hōjō Takatoki in 1316, it was the beginning of the end for the dominance of Kamakura. Takatoki was born in 1304 and was the son of retired shikken (regent) Hōjō Sadatoki. He became regent at the age of eight, so the real power was held by his grandmother, Adachi Tokiaki, and a minister named Nagasaki Takasuke, who was the head of the powerful Tokusō family.

When Takatoki was twenty-three, he fell ill and retired as shikken to become a monk, though he continued to hold considerable power within the shogunate. He did not appoint a successor, and the Adachi clan, represented by Takatoki's grandmother, and the Tokusō family, represented by Nagasaki Takasuke, supported separate candidates. The Tokusō were able to push forward their candidate, Hōjō Kunitoki, the infant son of Takatoki, but they needed an interim shikken to rule until Kunitoki was an adult.

They chose none other than Hōjō Sadaaki, the head of the Kanazawa branch of the Hōjō clan and a trader in tea. Sadaaki had brought his branch of the family to new heights with cunning political savvy, but his appointment was opposed by the Adachi and because of rumors of an assassination plot. In fact, Sadaaki had requested to retire from politics and become a monk like Takatoki, but he was denied each time. In the face of this open opposition, Sadaaki resigned as regent after only ten days on the job.

He was replaced by Hōjō Moritoki, who was associated with the Akahashi line of the Hōjō clan. Moritoki was to be another interim regent, and he was nothing more than a puppet controlled by Nagasaki Takasuke and the retired regent Hōjō Takatoki. Moritoki became regent in 1326 and held the position until 1333, which was when matters took a drastic turn regarding Emperor Go-Daigo.

In 1324, Emperor Go-Daigo was discovered to be planning an overthrow of the shogunate in Kamakura to restore the imperial family as the leaders of Japan. The shogunate stopped the emperor's plans, but Go-Daigo once again was discovered to be planning to overthrow Kamakura in 1331 after he was betrayed by his close associate, Fujiwara Sadafusa. Go-Daigo was exiled to the Oki Islands. A new emperor, Go-Kōgon, was installed in his place.

However, after two years, Go-Daigo escaped with the help of Nawa Nagatoshi. The two gathered an army to face the shogunate forces, led by Sasaki Kiyotaka, at the Battle of Mount Senjō. The imperial forces were victorious, which caused leaders to switch sides and support Go-Daigo.

The Hōjō clan then dispatched two forces to suppress Go-Daigo's uprising. One, led by Hōjō Takaie, was defeated along the San'yōdō route. The other, commanded by Ashikaga Takauji, turned against the shogunate and joined the imperial side. The reason for Takauji's defection remains uncertain, but it is often attributed to his status as head of the Minamoto clan, a traditional rival of the Taira. The Hōjō had maintained a long-standing alliance with the Taira lineage, dating back to the Genpei War.

Takauji quickly took control of Kyoto. Nitta Yoshisada, head of the Nitta clan, joined the emperor's side and laid siege to Kamakura. When the city fell, Hōjō Takatoki and his entire family committed suicide. The Hōjō clan was almost entirely wiped out, ending the Kamakura shogunate in what would be known as the Genkō War.

Emperor Go-Daigo returned to Kyoto and claimed the Chrysanthemum Throne, which began a brief period known as the Kenmu Restoration. Go-Daigo hoped to return Japan to a civilian government after many generations of military rule under the Kamakura shogunate.

Emperor Go-Daigo.*

However, the emperor displeased the warrior class by not rewarding them sufficiently for their support. The Hōjō lands that were seized were handed out to Ashikaga Takauji and Nitta Yoshisada for their efforts, and the rest mainly went to imperial favorites. The minor warriors who had supported the emperor were ignored, and they quickly became incensed. Important positions were given to nobles and bureaucrats. By 1335, the emperor had completely lost the support of the samurai.

In order to reestablish rule in Kamakura and the east without naming another shogun, Go-Daigo sent his young son to the east and named him governor-general of Mutsu and Dewa Provinces. Tadayoshi, the younger brother of Ashikaga Takauji, then took another son of the emperor and installed him as governor of Kōzuke Province in Kamakura. Tadayoshi's actions were not, however, ordered by the emperor. This disobedience went unchecked because the emperor did not have the resources to attack the Ashikaga clan.

In due time, the Ashikaga brothers, especially Takauji, came to represent the growing discontent of the samurai. With their support, he rebelled against Go-Daigo in 1336. Their forces met in the famous Battle of Minatogawa. Ashikaga's army was victorious, and Go-Daigo fled to Yoshino, where he established the Southern Court. Ashikaga Takauji placed Emperor Kōmyō, from the senior line of the imperial family, on the throne of the Northern Court. This divide between Northern and Southern Courts would last until 1392, a span of time known as the Nanboku-chō period. Ashikaga Takauji became shogun in the north, establishing the Ashikaga bakufu, or military government, in Kyoto.

Summary Timeline — The Kamakura Conflict

- 1200 CE (approx.) – Birth of Dōgen, later founder of the Sōtō Zen school in Japan.
- 1223 CE – Dōgen travels to China to study Chan Buddhism; trains under Rujing.
- 1253 CE – Death of Dōgen after establishing Eihei-ji Temple, a main center of Sōtō Zen practice.
- 1284 CE – Death of Hōjō Tokimune; succeeded by his son Sadatoki.
- 1301 CE – Emperor Go-Nijō ascends the throne; Hōjō Morotoki serves as regent.
- 1311 CE – Death of Morotoki
- 1316 CE – Hōjō Takatoki (age eight) becomes regent.
- 1316 CE – Beginning of Takatoki's regency; growing factionalism among Hōjō branches.
- 1324 CE – Emperor Go-Daigo's plot to overthrow the Kamakura shogunate discovered.
- 1331 CE – Go-Daigo again attempts rebellion; captured and exiled to the Oki Islands.
- 1333 CE – Go-Daigo escapes; allies with Nitta Yoshisada and Ashikaga Takauji. Kamakura falls; Hōjō Takatoki and family commit suicide. End of the Kamakura shogunate.

- 1333–1336 CE – Go-Daigo restores imperial rule during the Kenmu Restoration.
- 1336 CE – Ashikaga Takauji rebels against Go-Daigo; Battle of Minatogawa.
- 1336 CE – Takauji establishes the Northern Court in Kyoto; Go-Daigo flees to Yoshino, founding the Southern Court. Beginning of the Nanboku-chō (Northern and Southern Courts) period.

Chapter 5: The Ashikaga Era

Ashikaga Takauji.'

If Takauji had hoped that his time as shogun would be peaceful, he was soon proved severely mistaken. The existence of the Southern Court and the fact that Go-Daigo still held the imperial regalia would remain an issue for the rest of Takauji's life. In 1339, one year after Takauji had declared himself shogun, Go-Daigo died, and the throne went to Crown Prince Norinaga, who became Emperor Go-Murakami. For almost ten years, Go-Murakami ruled in Yoshino while Kōmyō ruled with Ashikaga support in Kyoto.

Then, in the early 1350s, a samurai general and shitsuji (shogun's deputy) named Kō no Moronao launched a campaign against the Southern Court. Emperor Go-Murakami fled his capital, but the Ashikaga forces were unable to capture Yoshino. The next year, Kō no Moronao, who was known for his violent ways and bad temper, quarreled with Ashikaga Takauji's younger brother, Tadayoshi. This led to a rift between the two brothers. Tadayoshi went as far, according to some sources, as to order Moronao's assassination, though it failed. Tadayoshi was then banished from the Northern Court despite having ruled in his brother's stead for years.

In 1351, Tadayoshi became a monk, but instead of retiring, he joined the Southern Court. Emperor Go-Murakami made him general over all the imperial troops. Tadayoshi was a skilled general, and in short order, he captured Kyoto and executed Kō no Moronao and his brother in Settsu Province.

However, Takauji gained the upper hand and defeated his younger brother at Sattayama. The brothers were briefly reconciled before hostilities broke out again, and Tadayoshi was captured in 1352. He died in prison, possibly from poisoning. The two courts remained, with Emperor Go-Kōgon in the Northern Court and Emperor Go-Murakami still on the throne of the Southern Court.

From 1352 to 1357, Takauji had to flee Kyoto multiple times due to invading forces. Each time, the Northern Court was able to recapture Kyoto. Kamakura was also captured and retaken once during this period.

Then, in 1358, Ashikaga Takauji died of illness. He was succeeded by his son, Ashikaga Yoshiakira, whose rule until 1367 saw further strife but also an attempt to consolidate power in the Ashikaga (also called Muromachi) shogunate.

This centered around noble lords known as shugo, who administered areas of Japan, though they remained in **competition** with the samurai in their districts. Yoshiakira and his deputy (*kanrei*), Hosokawa Yoriyuki, integrated the shugo into the shogun government. Hosokawa Yoriyuki held the title of Kyoto kanrei, which had supplanted the previous office of shitsuji (shogun's deputy). In an effort to balance the power of the kanrei, Yoriyuki proposed that the three head shugo families of the time—Hosokawa, Shiba, and Hatakeyama—alternate appointments as kanrei.

In 1368, Ashikaga Yoshiakira was on his deathbed and entrusted the care of his son, Ashikaga Yoshimitsu, to Hosokawa Yoriyuki. When Yoshiakira died, ten-year-old Ashikaga Yoshimitsu became shogun.

That same year, Emperor Chōkei ascended the throne of the Southern Court. Chōkei devised a plan to attack the Ashikaga in Kyoto from both the east and south. However, in 1369, the great imperialist general and hero, Kusunoki Masanori, who had captured and been driven out of Kyoto on four separate occasions, abandoned the Southern Court and looked for a peaceful way to end the dispute between the shogun and emperor.

Kusunoki Masanori was not an ordinary general. He was renowned for his loyalty, bravery, and exceptional personality. It was said that a samurai of the Akamatsu family planned to kill Masanori but committed suicide instead, not wishing to harm such a great man. His move to seek peace with Kyoto was seen as treason by many of those he had fought with, but he had grown tired of the constant quarrels of the Nanboku-chō period, and perhaps so had the people of Japan.

Masanori's apparent defection was also seen by some as the only means to save the Southern Court. If the young emperor continued with his planned attack, then the imperialist forces might have faced annihilation. There is reason to believe that the statesman Hosokawa Yoriyuki, the regent of the young shogun, also desired a peaceful conclusion to the war between the two courts, but it was not to be. In 1374, Chōkei abdicated in favor of his brother, Emperor Go-Kameyama.

The struggle continued for ten more years. Ashikaga Yoshimitsu became an adult and rejected the conservative rule of Hosokawa Yoriyuki, who returned to his home in Awa. In 1374, an actor, author, and musician named Kan'ami performed for Yoshimitsu in Kyoto. Many consider this to be the beginning of the Noh theater. "Noh" originally referred to any play that featured singing and dancing.

Two folk traditions were the roots for what would become Japan's predominant classical theater. Sarugaku was an ancient form of entertainment featuring acrobatics and farcical displays that eventually took on more dramatic features. Dengaku was the more musical of the two. Its name literally means "rice field music." To ensure a good harvest, people would dance and sing to the accompaniment of flutes and drums.

Sarugaku attracted more serious actors, while Dengaku became more focused on music, singing, and dance. Kan'ami was a Sarugaku performer originally, but he borrowed much from Dengaku performers. When he performed for the shogun, Yoshimitsu enjoyed the performance so much that he became Kan'ami's patron. He also showed special favor toward Kan'ami's son, Zeami, supporting his education and bringing him into court circles. Some later scholars suggest this relationship might have had an erotic dimension, though the evidence remains ambiguous.

The patronage of the shogun elevated their theater troupe and the actors themselves, who were originally from the lowest class of people, to a much higher status in society. Zeami wrote many of the treatises that would go on to define Noh theater. They were mainly based on his father's teachings and ideas about the art form.

In 1378, Yoshimitsu established the Flower Palace, which was known as Muromachi-dono or Muromachi Palace because of its location in the Muromachi district in Kyoto. Because of this, the Ashikaga period is often called the Muromachi period. Though this period was often violent and unstable, this era provided artists with the freedom to experiment and borrow from various other genres and art forms to create new and interesting experiences.

Yoshimitsu desired to bring more peace and stability to the nation, so he reorganized the "Five Mountain System" or Gozan Zen temples in Kyoto and Kamakura, as well as a network of lower temples throughout the country that acted as a kind of bureaucracy for the shogunate. This did not allow Yoshimitsu to regain control of the country, but it did establish a central philosophy of education since the temples often acted as the premier schools of the time.

The Nanboku-chō period, when the country was essentially split between the Northern and Southern Courts, finally came to an end in 1392. Yoshimitsu had been working tirelessly to promote the shogun's cultural **influence** through patronizing the arts and education and by strengthening his connection to both the imperial court and the shugo.

Part of this included persuading the western and central shugo lords to take up residence in Kyoto so they could be directly under his influence. The lords would then need permission to leave the capital, which was rarely granted, thus ensuring they could not spark revolts. Likewise, the shugo of the Kantō region were required to build mansions in Kamakura. While some lords were required to live in Kyoto or Kamakura, it became fashionable to do so, and lords who were not required to live there did so anyway. All the same, any lord who did not live in one of the capitals risked the chance of being branded a traitor.

Yoshimitsu also formed his own army of three thousand well-trained warriors, which could be supplemented by levying troops from the shugo. If a single lord was seen as becoming too powerful, the shogun was quick to put him in check with these forces at his command. They were incredibly effective at putting down a series of revolts in the late 14th century, namely the Toki Yasuyuki Rebellion (1389), the Meitoku Rebellion (1391), and the Ōei Rebellion (1397).

Yoshimitsu's preferred tactic was to pit a powerful shugo against a family member, which he did when he ordered Toki Yasuyuki to give up one of his provinces to a relative. Yasuyuki refused, and Yoshimitsu ordered the relative, Toki Yorimasu, to attack the traitorous lord. The resulting conflict saw the defeat of Yasuyuki, who gave up his province.

Yet, the real prize for Yoshimitsu was the merging of the separate imperial courts. Emperor Go-Kameyama became emperor of the Southern Court in 1383. After so many years of warfare and strife, the peace faction in the Southern Court, first begun by General Kusunoki Masanori, had grown more powerful. Yoshimitsu had also become interested in reaching an agreement between the two courts. Masanori, who died in 1390, never saw the peace he wished for, yet just two years after the hero's death, Emperor Go-Kameyama entered into peace talks with Ashikaga Yoshimitsu, thanks in large part to the shugo and clan leader Ōuchi Yoshihiro. He convinced the Southern Court to surrender. For this, Yoshihiro was awarded two provinces.

The Sacred Treasures, or regalia of the imperial court, were handed over to the Northern Court. Emperor Go-Kameyama abdicated in 1392 on the understanding that the throne would alternate between the Northern and Southern imperial lines every ten years going forward. The Northern emperor, Emperor Go-Komatsu, became the one hundredth legitimate emperor of Japan, according to the traditional line of succession. The two courts were now unified.

Yoshimitsu had accomplished much as shogun, and perhaps as a way to celebrate his success, he purchased the estate of the nobleman and poet, Saionji Kintsune, in 1397. There, Yoshimitsu built a grand palace covered in gold leaf. It would eventually become a Zen temple called Kinkaku-ji (Temple of the Golden Pavilion). Despite having been destroyed several times, it was rebuilt and remains a popular tourist attraction in Kyoto.

The year 1394 marked the beginning of the Ōei historic period. Japanese history is broken up into brief periods, usually only a few years long, that are typically marked by significant events. The Ōei period began with Yoshimitsu officially ceding his position to his son, Ashikaga Yoshimochi. However, Yoshimitsu did not actually retire. He remained very much in control of the bakufu (military government).

During this period, tensions between Yoshimitsu and one of his most powerful retainers, Ōuchi Yoshihiro, came to a head. Yoshihiro, lord of Suō and Nagato, resisted Yoshimitsu's demand that he contribute to the construction of a new palace. His refusal was taken as defiance of the shogun's authority. In 1399, Yoshihiro raised an army and fortified himself in the port city of Sakai, hoping to rally support against the bakufu. Yoshimitsu responded with overwhelming force, personally leading a massive army against him. The conflict, remembered as the Ōei Disturbance (or Ōei Rebellion), ended quickly. Yoshihiro was defeated and killed, and his rebellion was crushed by the shogun's superior numbers. The failed rising confirmed Yoshimitsu's dominance and further demonstrated the reach of the bakufu under his rule.

In 1401, Yoshimitsu sent an envoy to Ming China to reopen communication and trade between the two nations. The diplomats also brought a tribute of one thousand ounces of gold and precious objects. The Ming emperor, Yongle, replied the following year, granting Yoshimitsu the title "King of Japan," the only medieval shogun to receive this title.

In 1408, Yoshimitsu died suddenly at the age of forty-nine. His most long-lived legacy is perhaps his golden palace, which became the Zen Buddhist temple known as Kinkaku-ji, where a statue of Yoshimitsu can still be found. Upon Yoshimitsu's death, his son, Yoshimochi, took over as shogun.

The following year, Ashikaga Mochiuji became Kantō kubō, the title given to the shogun's representative in Kamakura, making it the equivalent of shogun in eastern Japan. The post had first been created in 1349, when Ashikaga Motouji, a son of Takauji, was appointed to govern the Kantō region. Kamakura remained the capital of the east, while Kyoto controlled the west. Though the Kantō kubō was in theory subservient to the shogun in Kyoto, the arrangement divided Japan into two overlapping centers of power. Eventually, the real power in Kamakura came to be held by the Uesugi clan, who served as Kantō kanrei, the deputies of the shogun in the east. Although Motouji was officially appointed to govern the region, he was often called the Kantō shogun or simply Motouji kubō. Since the shogun in Kyoto was also commonly referred to as kubō, Motouji came to be known as the Kantō kubō, a title that distinguished him as the shogunal representative in Kamakura.

Motouji died in 1367, and the title of Kantō kubō fell to his son, Ashikaga Ujimitsu. Even using the title Kantō kubō was potentially treasonous because it implied equal status with the shogun, but Ujimitsu openly desired to become shogun and clashed with the actual ruling shogun, Yoshimitsu. However, Ujimitsu could only aspire to this because he did not have the backing to challenge Yoshimitsu for the shogunate. Ujimitsu supported Yoshimitsu in 1391 against the Yamana clan, which won him more provinces. He never fully abandoned the idea of overthrowing Yoshimitsu, but he died at just forty-one in 1398.

The title of Kantō kubō then fell to his eldest son, Ashikaga Mitsukane. Mitsukane also openly aspired to the shogunate. In 1399, he planned to join Ōuchi Yoshihiro in his rebellion, the Ōei War, but he was unable to provide support before the rebellion was crushed. Since he had not actually participated in the rebellion, he was able to feign innocence when questioned by Yoshimitsu. He swore to support the shogunate in Kyoto, and peace existed between the capital and Kamakura until Mitsukane died in 1409. Then, his son, Ashikaga Mochiuji, became Kantō kubō.

Mochiuji was just a child when his father died, so the work of governing from Kamakura went to his kanrei (deputy), Uesugi Zenshū. Shogun Yoshimochi knew to keep a wary eye on the Kantō kubō and wait for any sign of rebellion.

In 1411, Yoshimochi abruptly ended his father's policy of engagement with Ming China, cutting off all diplomatic and trade relations. Yoshimitsu's acceptance of the title "King of Japan" had been controversial, as many in Kyoto saw it as submission to the Chinese emperor. Seeking to assert Japan's independence and restore domestic authority, Yoshimochi rejected the tributary relationship altogether.

Two years later, Emperor Go-Komatsu of the Northern Court, who had ruled for twenty years instead of the ten years originally agreed upon, reneged on the compromise between the Northern and Southern Courts. He handed the throne to his son, Emperor Shōkō. Supporters of the Southern Court were incensed by this disregard for the compromise, and hostilities resumed between them and the court in Kyoto.

By 1415, Mochiuji was showing a violent and abrasive personality. Uesugi Zenshū organized a revolt against his lord with the support of several shugo. By this time, the role of the shugo as military governors had grown. They dispensed justice, supported the shogun, and levied taxes on landholding nobles in their province. They also owned land; as land-owning warriors, they were called daimyo. The power of these "shugo daimyo" increased as the Ashikaga shogunate declined.

While Yoshimochi might have understood Zenshū's rebellion and might have liked the idea of getting Mochiuji out of the way, he had to send troops to put down the revolt. Zenshū had no right to defy his lord. The shogun could not let that crime go unpunished. His army finally surrounded Zenshū in 1417, and the kanrei committed seppuku instead of facing capture.

Mochiuji did not feel the death of Zenshū was enough, though. He attacked Zenshū's allies, the Takeda and Oda clans, as well as a few of the nobles of Musashi Province. He continued this punishment for several years, even though the rest of the Ashikaga clan felt as if he was going too far.

In the middle of this tension, in June 1419, the Joseon or Yi dynasty of Korea launched an invasion of the Japanese island of Tsushima. The *wokou*, Japanese pirates, had established themselves on Tsushima, and from there, they conducted repeated raids, not just on the Korean coast but also far into the mainland. The Ashikaga shogunate had been unable or unwilling to suppress this activity.

Korean armies had invaded the island and suppressed the pirates on two earlier occasions, but this had failed to solve the problem. The de facto ruler of Tsushima, Sō Sadashige, had managed to keep the island's pirates under control and maintain stable relations with Korea. When he died in 1418, however, authority on the island weakened. A pirate leader named Sōda Saemontarō seized power and led a massive *wokou* raid into Ming China. On their way, the pirates attacked the Korean coast and captured Cape Dodu on Jeju Island. Outraged, the Korean court declared war on Tsushima, and in 1419, King Sejong launched a full-scale invasion of the island.

The Korean invasion was led by General Yi Jongmu, who commanded around 230 ships with around 17,000 soldiers. After they landed in Asō Bay, Jongmu sent out emissaries to ask for surrender. When he received no reply, he ordered his men to raid and plunder the island's settlements. The sources offer mixed stories. The Korean records indicate they killed several pirates, freed Chinese captives, burned down houses, and captured several ships. The Japanese sources indicate that the Koreans faced significant resistance, mainly from the samurai of the Sō clan. Regardless, the Koreans left after a week and decided not to return. Tsushima and the Joseon dynasty entered into peace negotiations that eventually resulted in a treaty that allowed the Sō clan to monopolize trade with Korea.

In 1423, Shogun Yoshimochi resigned in favor of his son, Ashikaga Yoshikazu, who was eighteen years old. However, Yoshikazu died only two years later, so Yoshimochi returned as shogun. He stayed in power until his death in 1428 and was succeeded by his brother, Ashikaga Yoshinori. Yoshinori had been a Buddhist monk since he was ten years old, but he had been selected by the kanrei when Yoshimochi had failed to name a successor.

Not long after Yoshinori's succession, revolts broke out in several parts of the empire, including the Ōtomo Rebellion and the revolt of the monks of Mount Hiei in 1433. Yoshinori finally had the opportunity to strike out against the Kantō kubō, Ashikaga Mochiuji, who had been continuing his punishment of his perceived enemies. Mochiuji had grown too violent and too powerful to continue, and Yoshinori knew he needed to end Mochiuji's reign. Mochiuji's resistance would be known as the Eikyō Rebellion. The rebellion lasted several years, but in 1439, Mochiuji was finally defeated. He committed seppuku at the temple of Yōan-ji, west of Kamakura.

Despite not having been raised to be shogun, Yoshinori helped consolidate Ashikaga power and reestablished the trade relationship with Ming China, though his methods were often harsh and erratic. In one seemingly inconsequential decision, he made an enemy of Akamatsu Mitsusuke, who desired to be the head of the Akamatsu clan but had been overlooked by the shogun. Mitsusuke assassinated Yoshinori in 1441 and, in turn, was hunted down and forced to commit seppuku. The assassination of a shogun was almost unheard of and perhaps undermined the idea that Yoshinori reigned over a period of relative peace.

After Yoshinori's assassination, it was decided that his eight-year-old son, Yoshikatsu, would succeed him as shogun. However, the young shogun died in a horse-riding accident after reigning for only two years. He was succeeded by his younger brother, Ashikaga Yoshinari. Years later, the shogun changed his name to Yoshimasa, by which he is better known.

As Yoshimasa matured, a powerful rivalry developed within the shogunate. On one side was the daimyo Yamana Sōzen, who had become an ordained monk. However, due to his regular angry outbursts, he was known as the "Red Monk." Sōzen was jealous of his son-in-law, Kanrei Hosokawa Katsumoto, who, as one of the shogun's deputies, held immense power. The two waged a silent war, strategically trying to outmaneuver the other by interfering in the affairs of other families, most notably in the succession disputes of the Hatakeyama and Shiba clans.

In 1464, Yoshimasa expressed an interest in retiring as shogun. Since he had no legitimate heir, he adopted his younger brother, Ashikaga Yoshimi. However, the unexpected birth of a son to Yoshimasa a year later put the succession into question. Yamana Sōzen threw his support behind Yoshimasa's infant son, while Hosokawa Katsumoto pledged loyalty to Yoshimi.

It was at this moment that the war between the rivals turned from a silent battle of wits to an actual battle of swords in the streets of Kyoto itself. This was the beginning of the Ōnin War. The first battle took place around the Goryo Shrine. The battle was followed by looting, and a whole section of the capital was set ablaze. The younger members of the imperial family, along with most of the citizens, had been evacuated.

It was soon apparent that the nature of this war was one of destruction and ruin. After a month of fighting, most of northern Kyoto was decimated. Eventually, a stalemate existed in Kyoto, but the fighting spread into the rest of the country. Yoshimasa virtually ignored the war, instead being content with poetry readings and tea ceremonies.

In the rest of the country, the war that had initially been about the succession of the shogun devolved into battles between daimyo over land—power struggles that resembled the looting of burned-out Kyoto. The Red Monk and his son-in-law were both killed in 1473, but the civil war still raged on. Inter-clan fighting in Yamashiro Province, for example, led to a standstill between two factions of the Hatakeyama clan. The peasants and lesser samurai of the region revolted, expelled the Hatakeyama from the province, and set up a provincial government of their own.

The precarious order of the Ashikaga shogunate had toppled. While the Hosokawa clan held power over the Ashikaga shoguns, there was effectively no central power in Japan by the end of the Ōnin War. The daimyo ruled their respective provinces like kings over their own kingdoms, without answering to the shogun or the emperor. Japan had entered a new phase of history, the era of the Warring States, also known as the Sengoku period.

While the central government of Japan was crumbling, Japanese culture was reaching a new pinnacle. Under Shogun Yoshimasa and immediately following his death, many of the most quintessential Japanese art forms were formalized. The tea ceremony, a detailed and meditative ritual involving the preparation and serving of tea, became increasingly popular. Every aspect of the ceremony was prescribed and deliberate, from the utensils and movements to the setting in which the ceremony took place.

Along with the tea ceremony came the art of flower arranging, which was connected to the serving of tea. As was the creation of gardens with gravel raked into interesting patterns—what today is called a "Zen garden." Zen Buddhism, in fact, flourished at the end of the Ashikaga shogunate. Ink paintings also became a hobby of the elite, and Noh theater continued to dominate the entertainment of the wealthy and powerful.

This is just another example of the juxtaposition that seemed to be a significant element of Japanese history. While Japanese culture became more refined and ordered, the nation delved into chaos and violence. Yoshimasa was succeeded by his son, Yoshihisa, but he only remained in power for a few years before dying while trying to restore order in Ōmi Province in 1489.

Summary Timeline — The Ashikaga Era

- 1339 CE – Emperor Go-Daigo dies; Crown Prince Norinaga becomes Emperor Go-Murakami of the Southern Court.
- Early 1350s – Ashikaga deputy Kō no Moronao campaigns against the Southern Court, sparking conflict with Tadayoshi.
- 1351 CE – Tadayoshi joins the Southern Court, captures Kyoto, and executes Moronao and his brother.
- 1352 CE – Tadayoshi is defeated and dies in prison; the rival Northern and Southern Courts continue.
- 1352–1357 CE – Takauji repeatedly flees and retakes Kyoto; Kamakura changes hands as fighting spreads.
- 1358 CE – Death of Ashikaga Takauji; his son Yoshiakira becomes shogun and organizes the new Muromachi bakufu.
- 1368 CE – Yoshiakira dies; ten-year-old Ashikaga Yoshimitsu becomes shogun; Emperor Chōkei ascends in the Southern Court.
- 1369 CE – Kusunoki Masanori abandons the Southern Court, weakening its cause.
- 1378 CE – Yoshimitsu establishes the Muromachi (Flower) Palace in Kyoto.
- 1389–1391–1397 CE – Yoshimitsu crushes the Toki Yasuyuki, Meitoku, and Ōei rebellions, solidifying Ashikaga rule.
- 1392 CE – Reunification of the Northern and Southern Courts: Emperor Go-Kameyama abdicates and surrenders the regalia; Emperor Go-Komatsu recognized as the sole ruler.
- 1394 CE – Start of the Ōei era; Yoshimitsu cedes the shogunate to Yoshimochi but keeps real power.
- 1397 CE – Construction of Kinkaku-ji (Golden Pavilion), symbolizing the height of Muromachi culture.

Chapter 6: The Sengoku Period

A Sengoku period battle.⁵

Shogun Ashikaga Yoshihisa did not leave an heir, so he was succeeded by Ashikaga Yoshitane, his cousin. However, Yoshitane faced opposition from the powerful Kanrei Hosokawa Masamoto. Yoshitane was defeated by Masamoto and sent into exile. Ashikaga Yoshizumi was then made shogun, and in 1500, Emperor Go-Kashiwabara ascended to the Chrysanthemum Throne.

Yet, the powers of Kyoto mattered little to the rest of the nation. It became a time when people talked of *gekokujō*, or "the low dominating the high." Not only did the daimyo ignore the orders of the shoguns, but **commoners** began to oppose their lords. Farmers, monks, and lesser warriors would band together and revolt against their superiors. They established ikkō-ikki, or "leagues of one mind," which usually followed a religious leader whose followers were guided by a single-minded faith.

They were typically backed by the "True Pure Land" sect of Buddhism, known as Jōdo Shinshū. A priest named Rennyo, descended from the founder of True Pure Land Buddhism (Shinran), had the greatest influence over the ikkō-ikki. He challenged the power of the daimyo and other powerful Buddhist temples, such as Enryaku-ji on Mount Hiei near Kyoto. The monks of Mount Hiei led their own army, and during the Sengoku period, the government was unable to restrain them.

The Mount Hiei monks destroyed Rennyo's temple of Hongan-ji in 1465, though Rennyo was able to flee before the attack. He went to Echizen Province and established the temple of Yoshizaki-gobō. From there, Rennyo wrote and published works clarifying the True Pure Land teachings, which became known as Ikkō-shū, or the "single-minded school."

In his writings, he explained that Jōdo Shinshū was primarily focused on Amida Buddha and achieving rebirth in the Pure Land. In this primordial Pure Land, located outside the current reality, it is easier to reach Buddhahood and become completely enlightened because it exists beyond the corruption of the present age.

In 15th-century Japan, these ideas challenged the feudal structure of society and encouraged rebellions among the lower classes. Through the True Pure Land sect, these disparate groups could be united and organized in a way that allowed them to overthrow their local authorities—the provincial governor (**daimyo**) and the established Buddhist order (Tendai Buddhist monasteries).

Rennyo was a pacifist and taught pacifism, but he also recognized the tumultuous times he lived in. Because of that, any temples or monasteries he built were extremely well fortified. His followers, though, were not content to remain passive. They overthrew the governor of Kaga Province, creating the Kaga ikki, also called the "Peasants' Kingdom." They restored the shugo governor at Rennyo's request, but they soon overthrew him again in 1488 during what became known as the Kaga Rebellion.

The nature of the ikkō-ikki posed a serious threat to the economic and political supremacy of the daimyo. True Pure Land Buddhism would face near extinction by the mid-16th century. The idea that farmers, low-level priests, and provincial samurai (*jizamurai*) could challenge the authority of governors and established religious sects was intolerable to the high-ranking samurai and powerful monks. These men saw themselves as the true authorities of the Sengoku period.

By the mid-1500s, the power of these leagues had become impossible for ambitious warlords to ignore. Oda Nobunaga, seeking to unify the country, viewed the ikkō-ikki as a direct obstacle to his rule. He launched a series of brutal campaigns against their strongholds at Nagashima, Kaga, and Ishiyama Hongan-ji, destroying their fortresses and massacring thousands of adherents. These defeats shattered the military and political strength of the True Pure Land sect. Though its temples lay in ruins, the faith itself survived among the common people. It had been stripped of its armies but endured as a popular form of Buddhism.

Oda Nobunaga was one of three individuals who would rise at this time and become legendary figures in Japanese history. These three were, at times, allies and enemies, and their characters seemed naturally opposed. They were the three unifiers of Japan, and there is a set of similar stories about them that seek to explain their personalities and differences. The stories are all different, but they all make the same point.

In one story, the three men come upon a cuckoo bird that will not sing. Oda Nobunaga says to kill the bird, showing that he is a man of rash and violent tendencies. Then came Toyotomi Hideyoshi, who advised trying to placate the bird to sing. Then came Tokugawa Ieyasu. He explained that all they needed to do was to wait. Another story goes that Nobunaga gathered the ingredients, Hideyoshi cooked the meal, and Ieyasu ate it.

In the early 16th century, Oda Nobuhide was the head of the Oda clan and the deputy shugo of Owari Province. He had gained the nickname

"Tiger of Owari" for his ferocity and ruthlessness in war. Like other samurai lords in the Sengoku period, his life was governed by continual warfare with the other warlords around him. His chief enemies were Saitō Dōsan, daimyo of Mino Province, and Imagawa Yoshimoto, lord of Mikawa, Suruga, and Tōtōmi Provinces. The Oda were technically vassals of the Shiba clan, which formally ruled Owari; however, the Oda clan's power had come to surpass that of their shugo.

On June 23rd, 1534, a son and heir was born to Nobuhide. He was named Oda Nobunaga. This son of an embattled deputy governor of a small province in southern Honshu would go on to become one of the greatest figures in Japanese history. He is often called the first of the "Three Great Unifiers" of Japan.

In 1548, Nobuhide attacked Okazaki Castle in Mikawa Province. When the lord of the castle called upon assistance from Imagawa Yoshimoto, Nobuhide captured the lord's son, Matsudaira Motoyasu, who was just five years old. Nobuhide threatened to kill the boy, but even though he was defeated by Imagawa, he kept Motoyasu as a hostage.

In order to secure an alliance with his enemy, Saitō Dōsan, Nobuhide arranged for Dōsan's daughter, Nōhime, to be married to Nobunaga. This alliance held even when Nobuhide died unexpectedly in 1551. Even though Oda Nobunaga was Nobuhide's legitimate heir, his behavior at his father's funeral scandalized the clan. He arrived late, dressed in casual clothes, and threw incense at the altar instead of offering it properly. His lack of decorum shocked his retainers, who saw it as proof of his unfitness to lead. Many withdrew their support and turned to his younger brother, Oda Nobuyuki.

In response, Nobunaga gathered an army to put down any unrest and intimidate his enemies. Imagawa Yoshimoto, sensing weakness, laid siege to Anjō Castle, where Nobunaga's illegitimate half-brother lived. In order to save his brother's life, Nobunaga agreed to an exchange. He handed over his father's hostage, nine-year-old Matsudaira Motoyasu. Motoyasu would serve the Imagawa clan into adulthood.

Nobunaga then faced another challenge when his uncle, Oda Nobutomo, attacked part of Nobunaga's domain with support from the Owari shugo, Shiba Yoshimune. Nobunaga defeated his uncle and burned part of his castle at Kiyosu, but he left his uncle alive. In 1554, Yoshimune tipped off Nobunaga that Nobutomo was planning to have him assassinated. Nobutomo had Yoshimune executed, officially ending the Shiba shugo of Owari.

Just a few years earlier, Nobunaga had become one of the first lords of Japan to adopt a new type of weapon. In 1543, a Portuguese ship was blown off course by a typhoon and shipwrecked on Tanegashima Island. It was the first recorded European contact with Japan. If the Europeans found the Japanese fascinating, the **Japanese** found the Europeans very strange indeed. They called them *nanban*, or "southern barbarians," and while they thought their looks and dress were strange, they marveled at the items they brought with them, perhaps none as much as the matchlock firearms they carried. The Japanese called them *tanegashima*.

The Portuguese soon established trade routes to Japan, and commerce on the southern islands brought not just firearms but also wealth. And with that wealth came power. The new technology, particularly the matchlock musket, was quickly copied by the Japanese. Blacksmiths began to reproduce guns, with places like Sakai, Yokkaichi, and Kunitomo becoming famous centers of gun manufacturing. The Portuguese also traded in saltpeter, which was needed to make gunpowder, as well as silks, gold, and slaves.

They also brought Christianity in the form of Catholic missionaries, the first being Saint Francis Xavier, who arrived in 1549. Xavier was a co-founder of the Society of Jesus, known as the Jesuits. He had met a Japanese man named Anjirō, who had fled his country after being accused of murder. Anjirō led Xavier to Japan and acted as a translator and guide.

The Japanese were not easily converted. They questioned how a god that created everything, including evil, could be good in nature. They were also uncomfortable with the idea that their ancestors were eternally damned to hell.

The Jesuits found success by converting southern daimyo who desired to trade with Portugal. Those daimyo then commanded their subjects to convert as well. At first, the Catholic missionaries were tolerated, but their presence represented a threat to the power structure of the nation, which was closely tied to Buddhism and Shinto beliefs.

By the early 1550s, Nobunaga had become one of the first lords in Japan to recognize the potential of firearms in warfare. Matchlock muskets became an essential part of his growing arsenal. Nobunaga quickly learned how to deploy these weapons effectively, organizing his infantry to fire in coordinated volleys so that their line of gunfire remained constant even while others reloaded.

He used this tactic in 1554 when he faced the Imagawa clan at the Battle of Muraki Castle. Nobunaga called on the assistance of his father-in-law, Saitō Dōsan, who sent one thousand samurai, which Nobunaga used to protect his domain from attacks by his rivals within the Oda clan. He then led an army of eight hundred infantrymen armed with spears and five hundred with muskets. They sailed south and then marched north to attack Imagawa forces at Muraki Castle. This Imagawa stronghold had been taken in Owari Province in clear defiance of the Oda clan's dominance.

Nobunaga knew that if he was going to secure Owari for himself, he had to evict the Imagawa. The steady gunfire frightened the defenders so much that they surrendered almost immediately, proving not just the effectiveness of the guns but also the skill of Nobunaga's military leadership. This bolstered Nobunaga's reputation, and with this victory, he stormed Kiyosu Castle, forcing his uncle to commit seppuku.

Less than two years later, Saitō Yoshitatsu raised an army and overthrew his father—Nobunaga's father-in-law and ally—Saitō Dōsan, who was killed in battle. Yoshitatsu made himself daimyo of Mino Province and ended the alliance with the Oda clan. This loss of support led to the defection of several of Nobunaga's retainers. They rose against him and supported his brother instead, Oda Nobuyuki.

Nobunaga defeated them at the Battle of Ino but pardoned the rebels and his brother, partly due to his own mother's pleas. The next year, however, Nobuyuki once again conspired to rebel against his brother. Nobunaga was told of the plot and feigned illness. When his brother and his entourage came to visit the supposedly ailing daimyo, Nobunaga had them all killed.

It was 1559, and Nobunaga had finally established himself as the uncontested ruler of Owari Province. However, he was still far from fulfilling his destiny as the unifier of Japan.

Oda Nobunaga.[6]

The long-time Oda enemy, Imagawa Yoshimoto, secured an alliance with the powerful Takeda and Hōjō clans in 1560. He gathered an army of somewhere between twenty-five thousand and forty thousand troops and marched toward Kyoto to take control of the capital. In order to do this, he had to cross Owari. Oda Nobunaga chose to stand in his way.

Yoshimoto placed his retainer and one-time Oda hostage, Matsudaira Motoyasu, in the vanguard of his army. The Matsudaira clan joined Yoshimoto's forces, and they quickly took Marune Fortress. Nobunaga's scouts reported that Yoshimoto's army had encamped in Okehazama, just outside the city of Nagoya. Nobunaga could only field an army of about two thousand to three thousand men, and he told his advisors that only a strong offensive could make up for their inferior numbers.

The land where Yoshimoto had camped was well known to Nobunaga and his men because they had played war games there in the guise of falcon-hunting parties. Nobunaga's forces attacked the camp during a thunderstorm in the afternoon. Yoshimoto's forces were caught completely by surprise. They panicked, and many attempted to flee. Yoshimoto was roused from his tent only to discover much of his army in flight or dying. He joined the fight but was killed, and his head was taken by an Oda samurai.

At the Battle of Okehazama, Nobunaga noticed the talents of his sandal-bearer, a samurai of humble origins named Kinoshita Tōkichirō, who is known to history as Toyotomi Hideyoshi—the second great unifier of Japan.

After Yoshimoto's defeat, the Imagawa clan was greatly reduced and would soon be destroyed by its rivals. Many lords loyal to the Imagawa abandoned the clan and followed Nobunaga, including Matsudaira Motoyasu, who had once been a hostage of Nobunaga's father. Motoyasu would be known to history as Tokugawa Ieyasu—the third great unifier of Japan. Nobunaga also forged an alliance with the powerful Takeda clan.

In 1561, Saitō Yoshitatsu, Nobunaga's brother-in-law who had killed his father to become daimyo of Mino Province, died. His son, Saitō Tatsuoki, inherited the province, but he proved to be a much weaker leader than his father or grandfather. Nobunaga saw the opportunity and began a campaign to conquer Mino Province.

Nobunaga relied heavily on his retainer, Toyotomi Hideyoshi, to encourage retainers of the Saitō clan to abandon their weak leader and pledge allegiance to the Oda clan. He accomplished this primarily through diplomacy and bribery. In 1566, Hideyoshi was instructed to build Sunomata Castle on the edge of Saitō territory. It was largely prefabricated and appeared to spring up overnight. It was intimidating and surprising to the enemy.

In 1567, Nobunaga was ready to attack Inabayama Castle, the headquarters of the Saitō clan. The so-called "Mino Triumvirate"—three Saitō generals who were expected to meet Nobunaga in battle—defected and pledged loyalty to the Oda clan instead. However, Daimyo Saitō Tatsuoki was still inside the castle, which was believed to be impregnable. A plan was devised for a small band of troops to climb the rocky slope of Mount Inaba, on which the castle was built, and gain entry. Then, they would open the gates from the inside. Toyotomi Hideyoshi was selected to lead this group.

Hideyoshi succeeded. After setting fire to the castle's gunpowder stores, he opened the gates to allow Nobunaga's army to enter. Saitō Tatsuoki either escaped and went into exile or was captured and spared. Regardless, the Saitō clan and its retainers were now under Nobunaga's control.

Nobunaga revealed his wish to conquer and unify all of Japan. He renamed the castle and the nearby town Gifu in honor of the mountain where the legendary Chinese ruler Wu Wang (King Wu of Zhou) launched his campaign to unify China. In 1567 and 1568, Nobunaga sent his general Takigawa Kazumasu to pacify Ise Province. He especially wanted the head of the Kitabatake clan, Kitabatake Tomonori, who had adopted one of Nobunaga's sons, under his control. Nobunaga also consolidated his power through a marriage alliance with the Azai clan of Ōmi Province.

Then, in 1568, Nobunaga was approached by Ashikaga Yoshiaki and his retainer, Akechi Mitsuhide, to intervene in the Ashikaga shogunate in Kyoto. At the time, the Miyoshi clan effectively controlled the shogunate and had forced Yoshiaki's brother, the thirteenth shogun Ashikaga Yoshiteru, to commit suicide in 1565. Ashikaga Yoshihide was then installed as the fourteenth shogun. However, they were unable to gain control of the capital, and Yoshihide never entered Kyoto.

Nobunaga agreed to help install Yoshiaki as shogun and began his campaign to march on Kyoto. First, he faced the Rokkaku clan of southern Ōmi Province, led by Rokkaku Yoshikata. Nobunaga's forces quickly drove the Rokkaku from their castles and defeated them in battle. Nobunaga then entered Kyoto, drove out the Miyoshi who remained there, and installed Yoshiaki as the fifteenth shogun.

Nobunaga refused to take the title of kanrei or any other appointment from Yoshiaki. He asked the new shogun to call all daimyo to the capital for a banquet. The shogun's regent, Asakura Yoshikage, refused, so Nobunaga labeled him a rebel. This caused a rift between the shogun and Nobunaga. Yoshiaki began to secretly form an alliance with the Asakura clan and Azai Nagamasa, who broke his alliance with the Oda. They also enlisted help from the Rokkaku clan, the Miyoshi, and even the ikkō-ikki (armed military leagues).

The alliance drove the Oda forces back and led to the decisive Battle of Anegawa in 1570. Nobunaga joined his forces with those of Tokugawa Ieyasu and faced the Asakura-Azai alliance across the shallow Ane River. Toyotomi Hideyoshi led troops in battle for the first time. The fighting was fierce, but Nobunaga's forces prevailed and sent the enemy into retreat. Both leaders of the Azai and Asakura clans later committed seppuku, ending this brief anti-Nobunaga alliance.

Nobunaga then faced the ikkō-ikki alliances, which challenged his dream of unification. His first attempt was a failure, but he then focused on a siege of the warrior monks of Enryaku-ji on Mount Hiei. Much has been made of the burning of temples and shrines on Mount Hiei, as well as the deaths of up to four thousand monks, women, and children, whom Nobunaga was said to have ordered killed. Careful examination of the source material, along with archaeological work done at the end of the 20th century, suggests this was an exaggeration. Nobunaga's forces defeated the monks and certainly set fire to two of the largest buildings, but many of the residents of Mount Hiei had already evacuated down the mountain by the time the assault began. The death toll recorded by Jesuit priest Luís Fróis—about 1,500—is probably more accurate.

More devastating was Nobunaga's siege of Nagashima and the ikkō-ikki who controlled it. He tried to besiege the fortress on three separate occasions but was only successful on the final attempt in 1574, when his forces surrounded the stronghold and set it on fire. This resulted in the deaths of possibly tens of thousands.

The ikkō-ikki's main headquarters was the temple-fortress of Ishiyama Hongan-ji, which Nobunaga besieged from 1570 to 1580. In 1573, Nobunaga had ousted Shogun Ashikaga Yoshiaki from power. Yoshiaki, now in exile, helped supply the ikkō-ikki in Ishiyama and even raised troops to fight Nobunaga's forces near the fortress. He also requested aid from the powerful western Mōri clan.

Nobunaga changed tactics. He attacked fortresses near Ishiyama and succeeded in cutting the Mōri supply lines. By 1580, the siege had turned in Nobunaga's favor. The abbot Kōsa (Kennyo) and his sons finally surrendered the fortress, and the fighting ended. Nobunaga spared many of the defenders but burned the complex to the ground. The site would later be chosen by Toyotomi Hideyoshi for the construction of Osaka Castle.

While Nobunaga battled the ikkō-ikki, he was also contending with daimyo across Japan, wrestling for control of various provinces. His greatest foes were the Uesugi, Takeda, and Mōri clans. He gained dominance over these clans and took Iga Province in 1581. He was now at the height of his power and had become the de facto leader of Japan. He defeated the Takeda at the Battle of Tenmokuzan in 1582, which led to the death of their leader, Takeda Katsuyori.

Akechi Mitsuhide, the former bodyguard to Shogun Ashikaga Yoshiaki, had become a trusted general of Nobunaga. In 1582, he marched to Kyoto, ostensibly under Nobunaga's orders, when he decided to assassinate the warlord for reasons that remain uncertain. Nobunaga was staying at the temple of Honnō-ji in Kyoto with a few guards. Mitsuhide and his forces surrounded the temple. Seeing no other option, Oda Nobunaga, the first great unifier of Japan, committed seppuku.

Mitsuhide attempted to take power, but he was met by the Oda clan's forces under Toyotomi Hideyoshi at the Battle of Yamazaki. The night before the battle, Hideyoshi's generals, Nakamura Kazuuji and Horio Yoshiharu, sent a group of shinobi or "ninja" into Mitsuhide's camp to cause confusion and fear, robbing the enemy of sleep.

Ninjas, or shinobi, were covert agents used during the Sengoku period to gather intelligence, carry out sabotage, and spread fear among enemy troops. They came from regions like Iga and Kōga, where local warriors developed skills in stealth and irregular warfare. Unlike samurai, they operated outside the codes of battlefield honor, using disguise, infiltration, and psychological tactics. The group of shinobi sent into Mitsuhide's camp before the Battle of Yamazaki likely aimed to unsettle the soldiers, creating confusion during the night to weaken their readiness for combat.

Hideyoshi's forces defeated Mitsuhide's men, who fled the battle. Mitsuhide was killed by bandits while attempting to escape. Hideyoshi then summoned the daimyo to Kiyosu Castle to determine Nobunaga's successor. Hideyoshi was able to handpick the heir, choosing Nobunaga's infant grandson, Oda Hidenobu. A council of four generals was appointed to assist in governing.

Hideyoshi gained more power, receiving the title kampaku (chief imperial advisor) in 1585. He was at odds with Tokugawa Ieyasu, who attempted to check his growing influence. Rather than oppose him openly, Ieyasu submitted to Hideyoshi the following year, but on terms that allowed him to keep control of his eastern provinces. While other daimyo joined Hideyoshi's campaigns across Japan, Ieyasu stayed in his own domain, quietly strengthening his position.

Like Nobunaga, Hideyoshi never assumed the title of shogun. He continued his predecessor's work of unifying Japan, waging the Negoro-ji, Shikoku, Etchū (Toyama), and Kyūshū campaigns between 1585 and 1587.

Hideyoshi **banned** peasants from owning swords and began a nationwide sword hunt (*katanagatari*) in 1588. The confiscated swords were melted down to create a statue of Buddha. This effectively ended the peasant revolts.

Hideyoshi and Nobunaga's master of the tea ceremony was Sen no Rikyū, a Buddhist monk who helped develop wabi-cha, the most refined form of the tea ceremony. This practice emphasized locally made wares in place of ostentatious utensils and a focus on rustic simplicity. Rikyū became one of Hideyoshi's closest confidants. However, during one of Hideyoshi's angry outbursts, he was ordered to commit ritual suicide in 1591, possibly for political reasons.

Hideyoshi organized and launched a campaign against Korea in 1592. The invasion was initially successful, but it stalled with the arrival of Ming Chinese reinforcements. A second invasion in 1597 met with even less success.

On **September** 18th, 1598, Toyotomi Hideyoshi died, and the forces in Korea were recalled to Japan. His heir was his young son, Hideyori, but a new and decisive power would rise to finish the unification of Japan—the one-time hostage and seasoned general, Tokugawa Ieyasu.

Summary Timeline — The Sengoku Period

- 1408 CE – Death of Yoshimitsu; his son Yoshimochi becomes shogun.
- 1428 CE – Death of Yoshimochi; Ashikaga Yoshinori chosen as shogun.
- 1441 CE – Yoshinori assassinated; Ashikaga Yoshikatsu (age eight) succeeds.
- 1443 CE – The Ōnin War begins over succession disputes of the shogunate.

- 1449 CE – Yoshikatsu dies; Ashikaga Yoshimasa becomes shogun.
- 1467–1477 CE – Ōnin War devastates Kyoto and ends centralized authority; start of the Sengoku ("Warring States") period.
- 1489 CE – Death of Yoshimasa; Ashikaga power wanes as regional daimyo rise.
- 1534 CE – Birth of Oda Nobunaga, future unifier of Japan.
- 1560 CE – Battle of Okehazama: Nobunaga defeats Imagawa Yoshimoto.
- 1568 CE – Nobunaga enters Kyoto and installs Ashikaga Yoshiaki as shogun, effectively controlling the capital.
- 1573 CE – Nobunaga expels Yoshiaki; end of the Ashikaga shogunate.
- 1582 CE – Nobunaga dies at Honnō-ji; Toyotomi Hideyoshi avenges him and consolidates power.
- 1587 CE – Hideyoshi bans Christian missionaries and asserts control over Kyūshū.
- 1592–1598 CE – Hideyoshi's Korean campaigns drain resources and weaken his regime.
- 1598 CE – Death of Hideyoshi; Tokugawa Ieyasu begins consolidating power.

Chapter 7: The Peaceful Edo Period

Tokugawa Ieyasu.[7]

He was born Matsudaira Takechiyo, later known as Matsudaira Motoyasu. Around 1566, he changed his name to Matsudaira Ieyasu. After he had gained control of Mikawa Province, he petitioned the imperial court to recognize a new family name, "Tokugawa," after the area from which his ancestors originated. He provided proof of descent from the ancient Minamoto clan. Thus, he came to be known as Tokugawa Ieyasu. He remained an ally of Oda Nobunaga, even after the warlord accused Ieyasu's wife and eldest son of treason and had them executed in 1579.

After Nobunaga's death and the rise of Toyotomi Hideyoshi, Ieyasu was assigned lands in the Kantō region, far from Kyoto. He established his base in the small fishing village of Edo (the site of modern Tokyo). When Hideyoshi died in 1598, Ieyasu became one of the appointed guardians of Hideyoshi's young son, Toyotomi Hideyori.

Unsurprisingly, a civil war soon broke out after Hideyoshi's death. Ieyasu was the most powerful warlord in Japan and was, therefore, in an excellent position to seize power. However, he faced strong opposition from Ishida Mitsunari, a former vassal of Hideyoshi.

Mitsunari's support came from daimyo in parts of northern and southern Japan but predominantly from the west, so his army came to be called the Western Army. Ieyasu's influence was widespread, especially in central and eastern Japan, and his coalition became known as the Eastern Army.

This led to the Battle of Sekigahara on October 21st, 1600, one of the largest and most decisive battles in Japanese history. Ieyasu's forces numbered about 75,000, while Mitsunari's numbered roughly 120,000. Ieyasu gained the upper hand—once again, a decisive factor was the effective use of firearms. Mitsunari escaped the battlefield, but he was captured by villagers near Mount Ibuki and later executed in Kyoto.

This victory paved the way for a massive shift in the power structure of Japan and resulted in Tokugawa Ieyasu being named shogun in 1603 by Emperor Go-Yōzei. The Tokugawa shogunate was mutually beneficial to both the imperial court and Ieyasu. It gave Tokugawa Ieyasu the official sanction that Nobunaga and Hideyoshi had lacked, and in return, Ieyasu replenished the depleted imperial treasury.

Ieyasu was sixty years old, having outlived the other great men of his age. He used his time as shogun to consolidate and solidify his bakufu. This began the Edo period of Japanese history, which is referred to as such because Ieyasu was based in the city of Edo.

Ieyasu retired as shogun in 1605, but he remained the effective ruler of Japan until his death in 1616. His son, Tokugawa Hidetada, succeeded him as shogun, demonstrating that the new Tokugawa shogunate would be hereditary. Ieyasu focused on the construction and expansion of Edo Castle, which became the largest fortress in Japan. Edo became the de facto capital of the country, while the de jure capital remained with the imperial court in Kyoto.

Edo entered a period of rapid growth from the beginning of the 17th century to the beginning of the 18th century, rising from about 100,000 townspeople to more than 500,000 within that time. Including roughly 500,000 samurai and their households, the population likely exceeded one million, making it one of the largest cities in the world.

However, Edo was not the commercial center of Japan during the Edo period—that distinction belonged to Osaka. Kyoto remained the cultural and artistic center. The daimyo were required to live in Edo every other year under the alternate attendance system (*sankin-kōtai*), and a large number of ronin, or masterless samurai, came to live in Edo seeking employment. After the Tokugawa destroyed the Toyotomi clan in the Siege of Osaka (1614–1615), nearly 400,000 samurai across Japan found themselves without masters. The long peace that followed only increased their number, as daimyo reduced their retainers and dismissed extra warriors. Many of these ronin drifted to the cities, where they became a restless and sometimes troublesome element of urban society.

Edo was a heavily segregated city, with distinct areas for the daimyo, samurai, and the shogun's household. These were separated from areas for the merchants, who supplied them with the goods they required. There were districts for dye merchants, mat makers, cloth traders, horse-post makers, and so on. Many groups, such as ronin, homeless wanderers, theater troupes, and itinerant workers, moved through the city.

In later years, the Edo period would be viewed as a time when Japan closed itself off from the rest of the world. The term "sakoku" is often used, which means "closing the country." However, this term was not coined until the late Edo period and does not clearly represent the nuances of the more than two centuries of Tokugawa rule.

The Tokugawa were openly opposed to the spread of Christianity within the country and expelled missionaries or put them to death. Many Christian daimyo were forced to commit suicide under Tokugawa Hidetada and Tokugawa Iemitsu. Eventually, Japan shut down trade with all but one European power—the Dutch East India Company. Nagasaki became the sole port at which the Dutch and Chinese were permitted to trade with Japan. However, the Dutch and Chinese were not the only foreign powers in contact with Japan.

Japan also had extensive dealings with Korea during the Edo period. The ruler of the Joseon (Yi) dynasty was regarded as an equal to the shogun, so an amicable relationship was maintained between the two countries throughout those centuries. This was a particularly surprising reversal from the invasions of Toyotomi Hideyoshi (1592–1598), which upended much of the civil order in Korea and had ramifications on mainland China, as the invasions contributed to the fall of the Ming dynasty and the rise of the Qing.

However, Tokugawa Ieyasu and his successors took many precautions to smooth relations with Korea. In fact, one of the Tokugawa bakufu's main aims was to restore peace to a country that had been ravaged by civil war for hundreds of years. With this in mind, they limited contact with what they saw as the most disruptive powers in East Asia: the Europeans and, to a lesser extent, the Chinese.

They also developed policies limiting overseas travel and trade, called *kaikin*, or "maritime prohibitions." This was not only to secure peace within Japan but also to preserve the dominance and control of the Tokugawa shogunate. Japan was very aware of the Spanish conquest of the Philippines, which began in 1565, and sought to prevent the rise of any daimyo who might establish independent trade with a foreign power.

The Ryukyu Kingdom, a chain of islands south of Japan, had long been a tributary state of the Ming dynasty, but during the Tokugawa shogunate, the daimyo of Satsuma Domain fought a war against Ryukyu in 1609, making it a vassal state of Satsuma. This unique dual relationship allowed the Shimazu clan, who ruled Satsuma, to maintain indirect trade with China via the Ryukyu Islands. The actual economic benefits of this arrangement are debated, but the Shimazu used their control of the island kingdom to strengthen their position within the shogunate.

By avoiding direct relations with China and by severely limiting access for the Dutch, the Tokugawa bakufu ensured that Japan did not occupy an inferior position in any diplomatic relationship. This was crucial to a power structure that needed to assert itself as the final authority and avoid showing any weakness so an enemy could sow chaos.

In fact, Korea, though considered a partner of equal standing, did not interact directly with Edo but through the Sō clan of **Tsushima** Island, the closest Japanese territory to Korea. Unlike China and the Dutch, Japan had its own enclave in Korea, the *waegwan*, where trading took place. Likewise, Japanese merchants traveled to Ryukyu to conduct trade. The Chinese and Dutch merchants, however, were permitted to trade only at Nagasaki, though the Chinese were allowed to live in a small enclave within the city.

As a result, the expulsion of the Portuguese and the limitation of trade under the sakoku system did not lead to a shortage of imported goods. In fact, immediately following the expulsion of the Portuguese in 1639, the bakufu requested items from Ryukyu, Korea, and the Dutch in such quantities that an overabundance of imports caused a severe drop in prices, damaging merchants' profits.

One might wonder how Japan was able to purchase the imports it required, living on an island that lacked certain **resources**. The answer was silver. During the 16th and early 17th centuries, Japan was one of the world's leading producers of silver, with major mines at Iwami Ginzan, Ikuno, and Sado. Much of this silver entered China through trade. The Ming Chinese economy relied heavily on silver currency.

Eventually, the supply of silver declined, and in the late 17th century, Japan placed an embargo on silver exports from Nagasaki. Instead of silver, Japan increasingly traded in copper, which was of exceptionally high quality and soon made Japan one of the world's largest copper exporters. However, silver continued to be a major export from Japan through Tsushima into Korea long after the embargo was enacted. The Koreans would exchange the silver for Chinese silk, which, in turn, found its way into the wardrobes of Osaka, Edo, and Kyoto.

The traders of Tsushima used Japanese silver coins called chōgin for commerce because their purity—around 80 percent silver—was guaranteed by the bakufu. However, by 1695, due to a shortage of silver, the Tokugawa debased their coinage to 64 percent silver, which caused a significant decline in trade with Korea.

While the rest of the country suffered from inflation, the silver merchants of Tsushima faced the additional problem of a decrease in goods to sell. As a consequence, the entire domain of Tsushima, which relied almost solely on its trade with Korea for income, suffered greatly. The Sō leaders were eventually able to convince the bakufu to mint 80 percent silver coins exclusively for their use in foreign trade, not for domestic circulation, while ordinary coins continued to be debased.

Many of the restrictions on trade were passed by Ieyasu's grandson, Tokugawa Iemitsu, who became shogun at the age of twenty-one in 1623. He only truly came into power when his father, Hidetada, died in 1632. Iemitsu was known to practice the *shūdō* tradition of forming homosexual relationships with other men, a custom that was not unusual among the samurai elite. A later story claims that Iemitsu murdered one of his lovers in a bathtub, but the tale appears only in much later sources and is considered apocryphal by historians.

At this time, the imperial throne was held by Empress Meishō, who was the niece of Iemitsu. She reigned from 1629 to 1643.

In 1640, a Portuguese ship arrived in Nagasaki carrying sixty-one envoys from Macau. They had been sent to negotiate the reopening of trade. Iemitsu ordered that all 61 be executed by decapitation, and their heads displayed, as a warning against foreign encroachment.

Empress Meishō later abdicated in favor of her half-brother, Emperor Go-Kōmyō, who reigned from 1643 to 1654. Iemitsu died in 1651.

For the next two hundred years, Japan remained largely unchanged. The shogunate passed through the Tokugawa male line, sometimes from father to son or from elder to younger brother. Violence decreased, and rebellions became rare and swiftly suppressed. The shogun ruled as the ultimate authority in the country.

The Japanese government remained isolationist and conservative. Shoguns sometimes ruled by whim. The fifth Tokugawa shogun, Tsunayoshi (1680–1709), became known as the "Dog Shogun" because of his Edicts on Compassion for Living Beings (Shōrui Awaremi no Rei), which protected dogs and other animals in Edo. Yet, the role of the shogun hardly changed, and much of the governing of Japan was done through the bureaucracy of the bakufu. It was a time of peace and stability, but it was also a time of stagnation.

For nearly two hundred years, the quality of life for the average citizen remained almost completely unchanged. While turmoil rocked much of the rest of the world, it also brought progress through reforms and new types of government. Empires rose and fell, and trade routes spiderwebbed across the globe. Yet, Japan was, in many respects, untouched.

Still, it is difficult to argue that Japan remained completely unchanged. During the Edo period, the ukiyo-e art of woodblock printing and painting flourished. The dramatic arts, particularly kabuki, became immensely popular. Originally rooted in street performance, kabuki evolved into a sophisticated theatrical form that combined elaborate costumes, stylized gestures, and music to portray historical dramas and contemporary tales. Although women were banned from performing by the mid-17th century, *onnagata*—male actors playing female roles—became iconic figures in Edo's entertainment culture.

Poetry also flourished. The haiku, a highly condensed poetic form consisting of seventeen syllables, was refined under masters such as Matsuo Bashō, who elevated the form through his philosophical depth and focus on nature, travel, and transience. In the cities, playful and witty *senryū*—the satirical cousin of the haiku — circulated widely, offering commentary on daily life and human folly.

The military government of the shogunate took on more civil administrative features, especially after a series of bad harvests in the 18th century. Yet, taxes on commoners were fixed amounts and did not adjust for inflation. As a result, the financial resources of the daimyo dwindled over time.

While the shogunate tried to enact reforms to stop the migration of rural people into the cities, Japanese urban centers became among the largest in the world. During the Tokugawa shogunate, Edo was likely the most populous city in the world, with well over one million inhabitants by the early 18th century. Osaka, Kyoto, and Edo each had more than 300,000 residents at a time when only about 20 cities worldwide could make such a claim.

During the Edo period, a new nation had been formed and prospered. It was looking to expand its trade. This nation was the United States of America, and it was particularly interested in opening trade with the "closed country" of Japan. A whaling ship called *Manhattan* sailed out of Sag Harbor, New York, in 1843. Two years later, it rescued twenty-two shipwrecked Japanese sailors near the Bonin (Ogasawara) Islands. The ship was allowed to enter Uraga Bay, near Edo (Tokyo Bay), to return the survivors. It was the first time in more than 220 years that so many foreigners were permitted to approach Edo, yet the Americans were not allowed to land.

The Americans returned in 1846 when Commodore James Biddle entered Edo Bay with two warships, but his attempt at diplomacy was unsuccessful. Then, in 1853, US Navy Commodore Matthew Perry arrived with four warships. The Japanese called them the *kurofune*, or "Black Ships." After demonstrating the power of his cannons, Perry demanded that Japan open its ports to trade with the United States.

This marked the beginning of a new period called the Bakumatsu, which encompassed the final years of the Tokugawa shogunate. The country was split between those who desired to open Japan's borders and those who wished to remain a closed nation. At the same time, many factions sought to exploit the turmoil for their own advantage.

Despite the isolationist policies of the Tokugawa regime, Japanese scholars were able to study and apply advances in science and medicine through *rangaku*, or "Dutch learning." Through contact with Dutch traders in Dejima, Nagasaki, the Japanese learned of the Scientific and Industrial Revolutions taking place in Europe. They obtained and translated important books on a wide range of subjects. Japanese scholars kept abreast of developments in medicine, astronomy, and technology. So, while Japan was a "closed country," it was far from an ignorant one.

In 1854, the Americans returned, and under threat of force, the Tokugawa shogunate signed the Convention of Kanagawa. The shogun at the time was Tokugawa Iesada, the thirteenth Tokugawa shogun. Because the shogun was young and in poor health, the administration of government fell largely to Abe Masahiro, head of the Rōjū (Council of Elders). Abe was forced to confront the crisis of the "Black Ships."

In an effort to legitimize his decision, Abe polled the daimyo on how to respond to the Americans. The results were divided, which weakened the shogunate's authority. Yet the opinions of the Japanese mattered little in the face of Perry's overwhelming naval power. Japan simply could not match the strength of the American military at the time.

The resulting treaty, the Convention of Kanagawa, required Japan to grant peace and friendship to the United States, provide assistance to shipwrecked American sailors, and open the ports of Shimoda and Hakodate for resupply and trade.

Abe then sought to strengthen the shogunate by commissioning warships and artillery from the Netherlands. In 1855, Japan launched its first steam warship, the *Kankō Maru*. From 1854 to 1855, a series of devastating earthquakes struck Japan, including one that damaged Shimoda, one of the newly opened ports. Many regarded these disasters as signs of divine displeasure.

In 1858, the Americans imposed a far more unequal treaty on Japan, the Harris Treaty (Treaty of Amity and Commerce), negotiated by US Consul Townsend Harris. It opened additional ports, granted extraterritorial rights to Americans, and fixed low import tariffs. Similar treaties soon followed with Britain, the Netherlands, Russia, and France.

Uncontrolled trade caused a devaluation of the Japanese currency and destabilized the economy. A political crisis followed over the succession of the shogun, resulting in twelve-year-old Tokugawa Iemochi becoming the fourteenth Tokugawa shogun in 1858. As foreigners flooded into treaty ports, violence between samurai and outsiders escalated. Efforts to revise the treaties proved unsuccessful.

Japan was once again in disarray, and a new movement of reform began, not in the palace of the shogun or the mansions of the daimyo but in the imperial court. Emperor Kōmei had ascended the throne in 1846, and during the turmoil following the arrival of the Black Ships, he began to assert a moral and political authority that had not been seen since the Kenmu Restoration of the 14th century.

The fall of the Tokugawa shogunate would lead to the restoration of imperial power through Kōmei's son, Emperor Meiji. During this transformation, Japan would move from its feudal roots to a rapidly modernizing global power. It was the dawn of a new era in the "Land of the Rising Sun."

Summary Timeline – The Edo Period

- 1600 CE - Battle of Sekigahara: Ieyasu defeats western daimyo rivals.
- 1603 CE - Tokugawa Ieyasu named shogun; foundation of the Edo (Tokugawa) shogunate.
- 1614-1615 CE - Siege of Osaka: Ieyasu crushes Toyotomi resistance, securing Tokugawa power.
- 1616 CE - Death of Tokugawa Ieyasu; Hidetada succeeds him.
- 1632 CE - Tokugawa Iemitsu assumes power and strengthens national isolation.

- 1640 CE – Spanish envoys executed at Nagasaki; foreign contact further restricted.
- 1651 CE – Death of Iemitsu; succession continues within the Tokugawa line.
- 1700s CE – Peace and prosperity foster urban growth and cultural development in Edo.
- 1843 CE – American whaling ship *Manhattan* arrives; first direct foreign contact in centuries.
- 1853 CE – Commodore Perry's "Black Ships" arrive at Edo Bay.
- 1854 CE – Treaty of Kanagawa signed with the United States, ending national isolation.
- 1867–1868 CE – Tokugawa Yoshinobu resigns; Meiji Restoration returns power to the emperor.

Chapter 8: The Meiji Transformation

Emperor Meiji.'

The Tokugawa bakufu had proved unable to handle the pressure of the wave of foreign powers entering Japanese waters and ports in the mid-19th century. Each treaty technically required approval by the emperor, who remained the head of state, if not the leader of the government. Yet, many treaties were signed without imperial sanction or even knowledge. As the shogunate's power began to decline, imperial influence grew, though it remained limited to an advisory role.

In 1862, Charles Lennox Richardson, a British merchant traveling with friends, was murdered on the Tōkaidō Road near Kawasaki when he failed to dismount upon encountering the procession of Shimazu Hisamitsu, father of the daimyo of Satsuma Domain. The attack caused an international **incident** that led to the Anglo-Satsuma War of 1863, during which the British navy bombarded Kagoshima. The battle ended indecisively, but the Satsuma leadership agreed to pay reparations for Richardson's death and later developed friendly ties with Britain.

In the face of **such** incidents, the shogunate looked increasingly to the imperial court for advice on how to weather the political, economic, and cultural crisis. The country was in dire need of strong leadership and a clear vision. Emperor Kōmei saw the crisis as an opportunity, and a flurry of communication passed between Edo and Kyoto. Eventually, Kōmei summoned Tokugawa Iemochi in 1863. The shogun led a grand procession to the capital. It was the first time in 230 years that a shogun had visited a reigning emperor.

Kōmei also issued the "order to expel the barbarians" (*jōi chokume*) in 1863. Though the bakufu had no intention of enforcing it, the edict further undermined the shogun's authority and emboldened anti-foreign samurai, leading to a series of violent attacks on foreigners and shogunate officials. The British retaliated by bombarding Shimonoseki, which was held by the Chōshū Domain, in 1864.

The Tokugawa shogunate responded by sending an army to suppress Chōshū that same year. The matter was resolved when Chōshū leaders executed or expelled the samurai responsible for the uprising. The **Satsuma** Domain helped mediate the peace, and no major battle took place.

In 1865, Shogun Iemochi sought military assistance and technical expertise from Napoleon III of France, leading to the **dispatch** of a French military mission to Japan in 1867. The mission, composed of seventeen officers and instructors from various branches of the French Army, arrived shortly before Iemochi's death in 1866 and met his successor, Tokugawa Yoshinobu. Meanwhile, Satsuma had strengthened its relationship with Britain despite their earlier conflict.

The French, therefore, looked to support and modernize the shogunate, while the British and Americans increasingly aligned themselves with the imperial cause. The stage was set for a civil war. Both sides modernized their armies and adopted Western military tactics. A coup in Chōshū brought anti-shogunate reformers to power, prompting the bakufu to launch another punitive expedition.

This time, Satsuma entered into a secret alliance with Chōshū. Although both sides had modernized their forces, the Chōshū army was better equipped and organized. The ensuing battles resulted in a decisive defeat for the shogunate. Yoshinobu managed to negotiate a ceasefire, but the Tokugawa regime had been fatally weakened. It was unable to maintain peace or assert authority.

Emperor Kōmei died in 1867, and the crown passed to his son, Emperor Meiji. Meiji, first known as Prince Mutsuhito, was born in 1852, the year before Commodore Perry sailed into Edo Bay. His mother was Nakayama Yoshiko, the daughter of Nakayama Tadayasu. Tadayasu was from the Fujiwara clan and held the title of Minister of the Left (Sadaijin), which by that time was largely ceremonial. He was a close advisor to Emperor Kōmei and became Meiji's guardian upon his birth.

Tadayasu was among the growing number of nobles who had spoken openly against the "unequal treaties" with European powers, and he passed this belief on to his grandson. The slogan of the imperialist movement was *sonnō jōi*, or "Revere the Emperor, Expel the Barbarians," a reference to Emperor Kōmei's previously ignored order. In 1867, perhaps seeing his survival at stake, Shogun Tokugawa Yoshinobu resigned from his post and handed his governing authority back to the emperor (an event known as *Taisei Hōkan*).

This was the end of the Tokugawa shogunate, but the leaders of Chōshū and Satsuma were fearful that Yoshinobu would continue to exert authority over the daimyo. So, they claimed to have obtained an imperial order to move against him. Their armies entered Kyoto, where Yoshinobu had withdrawn. Tokugawa forces soon arrived, but they were denied entry into the city.

This confrontation turned into the Battle of Toba-Fushimi in January 1868, the first battle of the Boshin War (named after the era in which it occurred, 1868–1869). This war pitted the shogunate's remaining forces, which wanted to preserve the old government, against imperial forces seeking to restore the emperor's rule and expel the foreign influences that many blamed for Japan's troubles.

Yoshinobu abandoned his army once the imperial troops raised the emperor's banner. He retreated to Edo. His adopted heir, Tokugawa Iesato, later became head of the Tokugawa family, and Yoshinobu retired to Shizuoka Prefecture, just as Tokugawa Ieyasu had done two centuries earlier.

Emperor Meiji entered Kyoto and declared his restoration and the return of imperial power. He was just fifteen years old. His rise was orchestrated by Saigō Takamori, Ōkubo Toshimichi, and Kido Takayoshi, three samurai known as the "Three Great Nobles of the Restoration" (*Ishin no Sanketsu*) and considered the founders of modern Japan.

Saigō Takamori led the imperial forces, which were victorious in several battles and eventually surrounded Edo in 1868. The city and Edo Castle were handed over peacefully to the imperial army after negotiations between Saigō and the Tokugawa official, Katsu Kaishū. Despite small outbreaks of violence from Tokugawa loyalists, the imperialists were unquestionably victorious in the south, though resistance in the north, centered around the Aizu and Sendai Domains, continued for months.

Foreign powers remained largely neutral during the conflict. The imperial side promised to maintain foreign trade and protect foreigners in Japan, though some isolated attacks still occurred. Later in 1868, the remaining rebel forces in the north were defeated.

On October 26th, 1868, Edo was renamed Tokyo, combining the words "east" (*tō*) and "capital" (*kyō*). Tokyo became the new imperial capital. The Meiji Restoration had officially begun.

The new power in Japan was not so different from the old power. The emperor did not exercise much direct authority; instead, political power rested in an oligarchy composed of men from Satsuma, such as Saigō Takamori and Ōkubo Toshimichi, and Chōshū, including Kido Takayoshi, Itō Hirobumi, and others.

The oligarchy sought to modernize Japan through a series of sweeping reforms. Among the first was the abolition of the "four occupations" system (*Shi-nō-kō-shō*), which had divided citizens into samurai, farmers, artisans, and merchants. They also replaced the hereditary daimyo domains with non-hereditary prefectures, appointing governors (*chiji*) loyal to the central government.

A crucial element of the Meiji Restoration was the gradual abolition of the samurai class. The samurai were a massive financial burden on the new government, as many still received stipends from state revenues. These payments were a legacy of the feudal system, when warriors were supported by their lords in return for hereditary service. The Meiji government initially maintained the stipends to prevent unrest, but the cost quickly became unsustainable. To create a modern national army, the Meiji leadership introduced universal male conscription in 1873, ending the samurai's exclusive right to bear arms. Samurai were also prohibited from wearing swords in public after the Haitōrei Edict of 1876, which symbolically ended their privileged status.

While many samurai adapted to the new order, serving as bureaucrats, officers, or educators, others were discontented. A large number of these disgruntled samurai lived in Satsuma Prefecture. Although Saigō Takamori had been loyal to the Meiji government, he reluctantly became the figurehead of a major revolt against it. The imperial army defeated the Satsuma Rebellion, and Saigō committed suicide following the final battle at Shiroyama. However, he was later pardoned posthumously and remains revered as a national hero.

The Meiji Constitution was perhaps the greatest achievement of the Meiji Restoration. Promulgated in 1889, it established a constitutional monarchy that blended imperial authority with Western-style government institutions. The emperor was officially the head of state and the supreme commander of the armed forces, but real power lay with the Cabinet, led by a prime minister appointed by the emperor.

Japan thus became the first Asian nation with a parliamentary system, the Imperial Diet (Teikoku Gikai), which was modeled largely on the constitutional structure of the German Empire. Yet, Japan did not see itself as subservient to Western powers; rather, it viewed modernization as a means to stand equal with—and eventually surpass—the West.

A clear demonstration of Japan's new status as a world power came with the First Sino-Japanese War, which broke out in 1894. The Qing dynasty of China had also been attempting to modernize its military, but it was put to the test when Japan realized that Korea, which was still underdeveloped and unstable, posed a threat to its national security. Japan feared that Korea's weakness could invite domination by foreign powers, such as China or Russia, either of which could threaten Japanese independence.

After the Imo Incident (a mutiny of Korean soldiers protesting corruption and foreign interference) in 1882, **Chinese** troops entered Korea to restore order. This allowed China to exert greater influence in Korean political affairs. In response, Japan supported a pro-Japanese coup in 1884, known as the Gapsin Coup, which failed due to Chinese intervention. Tensions between the two nations remained high until they erupted into war in 1894, following the Donghak Peasant Rebellion in Korea, fueled by resentment toward corrupt officials and foreign encroachment. The Korean court requested Chinese military aid, which prompted Japan to send troops of its own. Although the rebellion was quickly suppressed, neither side withdrew its forces. Their standoff in Korea soon erupted into the First Sino-Japanese War.

At the outset of the war, most foreign observers expected a Chinese victory. The Qing possessed greater numbers and resources, and their Beiyang Fleet was one of the largest in Asia. However, the **Imperial Japanese Navy**, modeled on the British Royal Navy, and the Imperial Japanese Army, organized on the Royal Prussian Army, were far better trained, equipped, and coordinated. Japan also had a universal conscription system for men aged seventeen to forty. China was dealing with internal unrest, including rebellions in the north, which limited its ability to deploy troops effectively.

The first major engagement, the Battle of Pyongyang (September 1894), saw the Japanese surround and defeat a **Chinese** garrison. When China attempted to send reinforcements by sea, its fleet was decisively defeated by the Japanese at the Battle of the Yalu River. Japan then advanced into Manchuria and captured Port Arthur (Lüshun) and the Pescadores Islands, forcing China to sue for peace.

The resulting Treaty of Shimonoseki (1895) compelled China to recognize Korea as an independent nation, cede Taiwan and the Pescadores Islands to Japan, and pay a large indemnity. The victory marked a fundamental shift in the balance of power in East Asia. Japan had replaced China as the dominant regional power. China's defeat led to deep internal unrest and helped pave the way for later uprisings, including the Boxer Rebellion.

In the early 20th century, Japan engaged in another major conflict, this time with the other great imperial power in East Asia: Russia. The Russo-Japanese War (1904–1905) was fought primarily over influence in Manchuria and Korea. Japan again prevailed, though Tsar Nicholas II initially refused to surrender, fearing the humiliation of defeat. The war was finally settled by the Treaty of Portsmouth, **which** was mediated by US President Theodore Roosevelt, who later received the Nobel Peace Prize for his efforts.

Japan's victory solidified its position as the preeminent power in Asia and showed the world that a modern Asian nation could defeat a major European empire. Japan formally annexed Korea in 1910, further expanding its own empire. For Russia, the loss exposed deep weaknesses in the Romanov regime, **sparking** domestic unrest that led to the 1905 Revolution and, in the longer term, contributed to the Russian Revolution of 1917.

Japan's triumph over Russia inspired nationalist movements throughout Asia. Even in China, intellectuals **saw** Japan as proof that modernization could resist Western imperialism. The British were deeply impressed by Japan's naval victory at the Battle of Tsushima (1905). They often compared it to Admiral Horatio Nelson's victory at Trafalgar. They even sent a symbolic gift of a lock of Nelson's hair to Japanese Admiral Tōgō Heihachirō. Japan had shown the world that it stood as an equal among the great powers of Europe. Emboldened by its success, it sought to expand its sphere of influence across Asia.

Summary Timeline — The Meiji Transformation

- 1862 CE – British merchant Charles Lennox Richardson killed; leads to British retaliation against Satsuma.
- 1863 CE – Emperor Kōmei summons Shogun Iemochi to Kyoto for the first time in centuries; issues an order to expel foreigners; British bombard Kagoshima.
- 1864 CE – Chōshū Expedition: Tokugawa forces punish Chōshū Domain; peace brokered by Satsuma.
- 1865 CE – Shogun Iemochi seeks French military assistance.
- 1866 CE – Iemochi dies; Tokugawa Yoshinobu becomes shogun.
- 1867 CE – Emperor Kōmei dies; Yoshinobu resigns the shogunate and returns power to the emperor; Prince Mutsuhito (Emperor Meiji) ascends the throne at age fifteen.
- 1868 CE – Boshin War: Saigō's forces surround Edo; Edo Castle surrenders peacefully; northern rebels defeated. Edo renamed Tokyo and made the imperial capital. Beginning of the Meiji Restoration.

- Post-1868 reforms – Domains abolished and replaced by prefectures; samurai privileges ended; conscription law and social reorganization enacted.
- 1890 CE – Meiji Constitution completed and promulgated.
- 1894–1895 CE – First Sino-Japanese War; Japan defeats China and gains Taiwan.
- 1904–1905 CE – Russo-Japanese War, ends with Treaty of Portsmouth.
- 1910 CE – Japan annexes Korea.

Chapter 9: The Shōwa Era

Emperor Meiji died in 1912 and was succeeded by his son, Emperor Taishō, who had long shown signs of a neurological disorder. Emperor Taishō played a very small role in political affairs. After 1919, he performed no official duties. His son, Crown Prince Hirohito, became regent in 1921. Hirohito was born in 1901 while his grandfather, Meiji, was still emperor. He was a sickly child, and his education was focused on physical fitness and health.

Hirohito was commissioned into both the Imperial Army and Navy at a young age and became regent

Emperor Shōwa (Hirohito).⁹

when he was twenty years old. Around that time, he took a six-month tour of Europe and became fascinated with the West. He enjoyed European fashion and food, and the trip deeply influenced his outlook on Japan's place in the world.

While the emperor was involved in important decision-making and the nation officially revolved around him, the real power lay with the prime minister. However, the prime minister typically served a short term, sometimes less than a year. During the Meiji Restoration, Japan had adopted a European-style peerage system, and most prime ministers were viscounts or barons, though many came from humble beginnings.

Viscount Takahashi Korekiyo, who served as prime minister from 1921 to 1922 when Hirohito was regent, was the illegitimate son of a court painter. He traveled to California in the 1860s, where he worked as a laborer—some accounts even suggest he was briefly indentured—but he eventually returned to Japan. He showed great talent in finance, helping to secure funding for the Russo-Japanese War, and was later honored with the title of viscount for his service.

The first prime minister appointed by Emperor Hirohito after he ascended the throne in 1926 was Tanaka Giichi, president of the Rikken Seiyūkai political party. Tanaka ordered a series of arrests of suspected communists and pursued an aggressive military policy abroad. It was clear that nationalist elements in Japan were seeking to expand their territories. Tanaka also pushed a strategy to separate Manchuria from China, laying the groundwork for Japan's later control over the region.

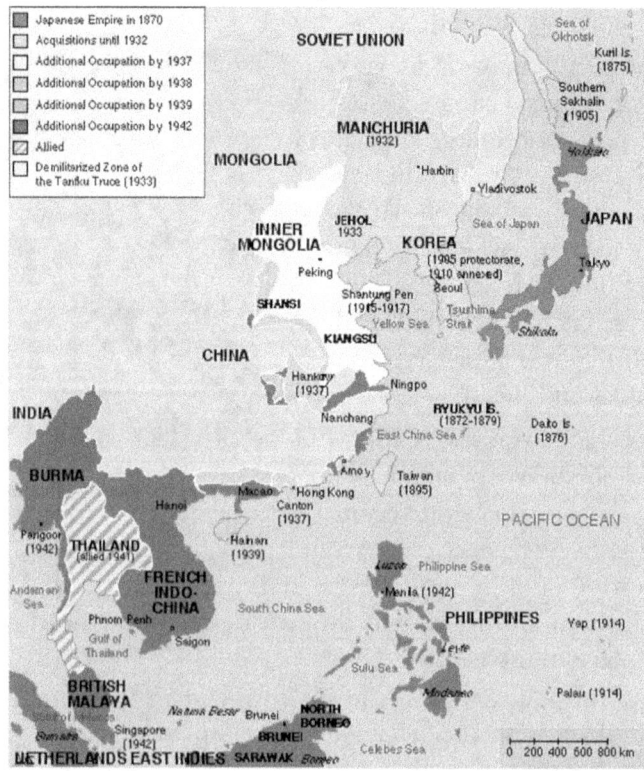

The expansion of the Japanese Empire.[10]

The Manchurian warlord Zhang Zuolin was assassinated in 1928 by junior officers in the Kwantung Army, a Japanese military force stationed in Manchuria. Although Zhang had once cooperated with Japan, he had begun to assert his independence, moving his regime southward and showing signs of reconciliation with Chiang Kai-shek's Nationalist government in China. This alarmed the Kwantung Army, which feared a loss of Japanese influence in the region.

Determined to protect Japan's strategic and economic interests in Manchuria, a group of radical officers orchestrated his assassination by bombing his train near Mukden. Prime Minister Tanaka Giichi was shocked by the incident but chose to cover up Japanese involvement, fearing political fallout and discord within the military. The failure to hold the perpetrators accountable not only undermined civilian control over the military but also drew the disapproval of Emperor Hirohito. After losing the emperor's confidence, Tanaka resigned in July 1929.

Hamaguchi Osachi was then selected to be the prime minister. Hamaguchi belonged to the Constitutional Democratic Party, or Rikken Minseitō. This party focused more on domestic economic reform than on the conquest of East Asia. Japan's economy was in serious trouble following World War I. Though Japan had been allied with the United Kingdom, fought the German Navy in the Pacific, and provided support to the Allies in Europe, the war had led to rapid inflation. The nation was facing rising debt, despite having gained former German territories in the Pacific.

The Great Kantō earthquake of 1923 had also worsened Japan's economic strain. The 7.9 magnitude earthquake caused massive destruction and loss of life in Tokyo and Yokohama. In the aftermath, rumors spread that ethnic Koreans were poisoning wells and planning attacks, which led to vigilante and police violence that killed an estimated six thousand to ten thousand Koreans in what became known as the Kantō Massacre.

The situation further deteriorated when the Great Depression struck soon after Hamaguchi took office. He responded with austerity measures, including significant reductions in military spending. However, his decision to restore the yen to the gold standard in 1930 worsened the economic crisis by making Japanese exports less competitive.

In November 1930, Hamaguchi was shot by a right-wing nationalist at Tokyo Station. Though he initially survived and was reelected while recovering, his health declined. He died of his wounds in August 1931.

He was succeeded by Wakatsuki Reijirō, who served only briefly before being replaced by Inukai Tsuyoshi. Inukai supported increased military expenditure and the expansion into Manchuria. He took Japan off the gold standard, which helped exports but further empowered the military. Despite Emperor Hirohito's requests to avoid escalation with China, Inukai reluctantly approved Japanese military operations in Manchuria following the Mukden Incident of 1931, though his control over the military was limited.

The Mukden Incident was orchestrated by officers in the Kwantung Army and involved the staged explosion of a section of the South Manchurian Railway near Mukden (modern-day Shenyang) on September 18th, 1931. Though the damage was minimal and train service quickly resumed, the army used it as a pretext to launch a full-scale invasion of Manchuria without prior approval from the civilian government in Tokyo. This marked a turning point in Japanese militarism, as the military increasingly operated beyond the control of elected officials.

Tensions between the civilian government and the armed forces rose sharply. In May 1932, Inukai was assassinated by a group of young naval officers in what became known as the May 15 Incident. His death effectively ended Japan's era of civilian leadership. Real power shifted increasingly to the military, and the prime ministers who followed were moderates who tried—but failed—to restrain Japan's growing militarism.

The culmination of the internal tensions in Japan was the February 26 Incident of 1936. A group of lower-ranking young officers from the Imperial Japanese Army conducted a coup d'état against the military and government, hoping to remove what they called the "evil" advisors around the emperor and the privileged classes they believed were ruining the nation's economy.

This group, numbering about 1,400 soldiers and roughly 100 officers, called itself the Kokutai Genri-ha, or "National Principle Faction." They were all heavily influenced by ultranationalist and anti-corruption ideals, and they believed they represented the working and lower classes against the entrenched elites.

Previous outbursts of political violence in which the perpetrators received light or no punishment convinced the Kokutai Genri-ha that, with proper organization and willpower, they could achieve the political change they desired with only a small number of men. In 1935, Lieutenant Colonel Saburō Aizawa murdered Major General Tetsuzan Nagata, a leading member of the rival "Control Faction." Though Aizawa received the death penalty, he was hailed as a hero by many in the Imperial Way faction, which only emboldened the Kokutai Genri-ha.

During the uprising, the conspirators assassinated former Prime Minister Saitō Makoto, Finance Minister (and former Prime Minister) Takahashi Korekiyo, and Army Inspector General Watanabe Jōtarō. Prime Minister Keisuke Okada narrowly escaped death when the rebels mistakenly killed his brother-in-law. The young officers were inspired by, and in some cases aided by, senior officers **aligned** with the Imperial Way Faction (Kōdōha), a radical group within the army that sought to restore imperial rule by purging corrupt politicians, bureaucrats, and senior officers.

At first, it seemed that the coup might succeed, as the rebels occupied key government buildings in Tokyo. However, Emperor Hirohito was furious and personally demanded that the rebellion be crushed **immediately**. This gave the rival Control Faction (Tōseiha) the authority to suppress the uprising. Within a few days, the rebellion was crushed, and the conspirators were arrested. The punishments were severe. Seventeen officers and two civilian ringleaders were tried in secret and executed by firing squad. With this, the Tōseiha Faction solidified its dominance within the army. More broadly, the incident further increased the military's influence in government affairs, as civilian leaders grew even more reluctant to challenge them.

Outside Japan, the military continued its policy of expansion, despite the disapproval of most Western powers. The Japanese Empire had already clashed with China in 1932, establishing a puppet government in Manchuria called Manchukuo, and had begun a campaign to suppress any armed resistance there. Following the Mukden Incident, Japanese forces quickly overran the region, encountering only scattered Chinese opposition. In 1932, they declared the creation of Manchukuo under the nominal leadership of Puyi, the last emperor of the Qing dynasty, though real authority rested with the Japanese military and civilian administrators.

The League of Nations condemned the invasion and refused to recognize Manchukuo's legitimacy, prompting Japan to withdraw from the League in 1933. Despite international criticism, Japan expanded its occupation, waging brutal counterinsurgency operations against Chinese guerrilla fighters and local resistance movements.

In 1933, the Japanese defeated Chinese forces and gained control of Rehe (Jehol) Province in Inner Mongolia. These actions were not the result of direct orders from Tokyo but rather the independent operations of the Kwantung Army, whose ambitions often exceeded official policy. This unchecked military activity led directly to the outbreak of the Second Sino-Japanese War, known in China as the War of Resistance Against Japan.

At the same time that Japan was entering into war with the rest of China, it was also mobilizing the emigration of Japanese farmers from the homeland to Manchuria. The original goal was to settle one million emigrants, but ultimately only about 300,000 made the move. The idea of others leaving for a new land was more appealing than doing so oneself, and many emigrants were **encouraged** or pressured to leave Japan.

The political climate in Japan was dominated by the increasing power of the military. The prime minister in 1936, Kōki Hirota, attempted to placate the armed forces by reinstating the rule that the Army and Navy ministers had to be active-duty officers. This policy, first introduced in 1900, effectively gave the military veto power over any civilian Cabinet. Hirota condemned some of the military's actions, but he did little to restrain them.

Hirota served for less than a year and was replaced by Senjūrō Hayashi, who had previously commanded forces in Korea and played a role in the Manchurian invasion following the 1931 Mukden Incident. Hayashi failed to form a stable Cabinet and served only four months before being replaced by Prince Fumimaro Konoe. It was during Konoe's first term that the full-scale invasion of China began.

On July 7th, 1937, a skirmish broke out between Chinese and Japanese troops near the Marco Polo Bridge (also known as the Lugou Bridge) outside of Beijing. The clash began during night maneuvers between local units but quickly escalated when both sides called for reinforcements. Neither the Chinese nor the Japanese government initially intended to start a war, but the confrontation spiraled out of control. Within weeks, Japan had launched a general offensive in northern China. This incident is often considered the true beginning of World War II in Asia.

Later in July, the Battle of Beiping-Tianjin saw the National Revolutionary Army of the Republic of China face the Imperial Japanese Army. The Japanese were victorious and took Beijing soon after. Japan justified its actions by claiming it sought to form a "unified front" against Soviet expansion and to resist Western imperialism, particularly from Britain and the United States.

Imperial Japan was openly opposed to communism, especially the growing power of the Soviet Union, and because of this, relations between Germany and Japan improved. In November 1936, they signed the Anti-Comintern Pact, an agreement directed against the Communist International (Comintern). By this time, Germany had been under Nazi control for three years. That same year, Prince Chichibu, Emperor Hirohito's younger brother, attended the 1937 Nuremberg Rally, where the Nazis declared the Japanese to be "honorary Aryans." Italy joined the pact soon after, marking the beginning of what became known as the Axis Powers.

With the outbreak of the Second Sino-Japanese War, Adolf Hitler abandoned his earlier cooperation with Chiang Kai-shek's China and declared support for Japan's campaign in East Asia, even though it meant conceding territories that had once been under German control before World War I.

In August 1937, the Battle of Shanghai began, pitting Chinese and Japanese forces in one of the bloodiest early battles of the war. The Chinese fielded around 700,000 troops, while the Japanese had about 300,000. The battle lasted until November 1937 and ended in a Japanese victory and the occupation of Shanghai. The success led to the decision to march on Nanjing (also known as Nanking), the capital of the Republic of China, which Japanese forces reached by December 1937.

What followed was the Nanjing Massacre, also called the Rape of Nanjing, in which the victorious Japanese forces committed mass rape, arson, murder, and looting over the course of six weeks. It is unclear who sanctioned the massacre—some sources refer to a "kill-all-captives order"—but the Japanese commander, Prince Asaka Yasuhiko, certainly made no attempt to stop it. Captured Chinese soldiers, as well as male civilians, were killed indiscriminately. The total number of those killed is impossible to determine, but estimates range from 40,000 to over 300,000, while cases of rape are estimated to be between 20,000 and 80,000.

The cruelty exhibited in Nanjing was not an isolated occurrence. Japanese soldiers committed numerous war crimes during the invasion of northern and central China. The exact reasons for these atrocities remain debated. Some historians point to the adoption of fascist ideology within the military, others to the dehumanization of the enemy, and still others to the brutal militarism of Japanese culture at the time. Undoubtedly, these actions were also fueled by racist attitudes toward other Asian peoples, whom Japanese propaganda depicted as inferior.

Prime Minister Fumimaro Konoe defended the campaign by claiming it was retaliation for Chinese aggression by the Republic of China and the Kuomintang Party. The Kuomintang's leader, Chiang Kai-shek, had actually proposed peace talks before the Battle of Nanjing, but Konoe rejected the offer. In later years, the Japanese government destroyed many documents related to the massacre and sought to downplay or deny the atrocities inflicted on the people of Nanjing.

The war in China continued until the Japanese army realized it could extend itself no further. In 1939, a stalemate had been reached. By that time, war had broken out in Europe, and World War II was underway. Despite Japan's alliance with Germany and its shared hostility toward communism, Germany signed a non-aggression pact with the Soviet Union in 1939—the Molotov-Ribbentrop Pact—leaving Japan diplomatically isolated.

In 1941, Japan and the Soviet Union signed a neutrality pact, while Germany prepared for its invasion of Russia. Meanwhile, Japan sought to resolve growing tensions with the United States. The US demanded that Japan withdraw from China, and in response to Japan's continued expansion, it imposed embargoes on key materials, most importantly oil.

Japanese leaders refused to abandon their conquests in China and recognized that their only access to essential raw materials—particularly oil and rubber—lay in Southeast Asia, especially the Dutch East Indies. Knowing that such an expansion would provoke war with the United States, Japan decided to launch a preemptive strike against the US Pacific Fleet.

Prime Minister Konoe resigned and was replaced by Hideki Tōjō. Konoe had attempted to negotiate a settlement with the United States, but talks stalled over Japan's continued occupation of China and Southeast Asia. Increasingly isolated within his own Cabinet and unable to restrain the military's influence, he stepped down, recognizing that he no longer had the authority to shape policy. His resignation cleared the way for the Minister of the Army, Tōjō, to assume the premiership and direct Japan more decisively toward war. Emperor Hirohito agreed to the plans for the attack, and on December 7th, 1941, the Japanese carried out a surprise assault on the naval base at Pearl Harbor in Hawaii. They simultaneously attacked Guam, the Philippines, Wake Island, and Hong Kong.

The Japanese hoped to cripple the US fleet long enough to establish their Southeast Asian empire and create defensive buffer zones. However, while the attack at Pearl Harbor was devastating, its long-term impact was limited since many of the primary targets, including three aircraft carriers, were at sea when the attack occurred. The attack on Pearl Harbor outraged the American public, who had previously been opposed to entering the war but now felt compelled to retaliate.

Japan captured Hong Kong by Christmas of 1941. In 1942, Japanese forces advanced down the Malay Peninsula and drove the British out of East Asian waters. They then attacked the Philippines and forced American forces to surrender, leaving around seventy-eight thousand American and Filipino **prisoners** of war. By February of that year, Japan had taken Singapore. They seized Burma, Java, Sumatra, and other islands that had once been part of the Dutch East Indies.

These victories, though rapid, came at the cost of overextension. By mid-1942, Japan's momentum stalled. The Battle of the Coral Sea in May halted its push toward Australia, and the Battle of Midway in June inflicted serious losses on the Imperial Japanese Navy, including four aircraft carriers. At **Milne** Bay in the fall, Australian forces repelled a Japanese landing, marking Japan's first major defeat on land. From then on, the Allies slowly pushed back against Japanese forces, island by island. The US retook the Philippines in 1944, and bombing raids on Japan itself soon followed.

Japanese forces fought with a doctrine that emphasized honor, discipline, and sacrifice. Surrender was considered shameful, both for soldiers and civilians. This mindset contributed to the ferocity of Japanese resistance, especially in the later stages of the war. Suicide attacks, including the use of **kamikaze** pilots who deliberately crashed aircraft into Allied ships, became increasingly common as defeat loomed. Civilians were often caught in the middle or mobilized for defense. By 1945, Japan was preparing for a final homeland battle.

The government remained divided between those seeking a negotiated peace and those insisting on continuing the war. One key obstacle was the fate of Emperor Hirohito, whom many leaders wanted to preserve as a condition for surrender.

In late July 1945, the United States and its allies issued the Potsdam Declaration, calling for Japan's unconditional surrender. It warned of "prompt and utter destruction," but it did not mention atomic weapons directly. Leaflets were dropped over Japanese cities in the following days, but there is no evidence that Hiroshima was specifically warned before the bombing.

On August 6th, the United States dropped the first atomic bomb on Hiroshima, killing tens of thousands. No surrender came. On August 8th, the Soviet Union declared war on Japan and invaded Manchuria. The very next day, the US dropped a second atomic bomb on Nagasaki. The government still hesitated, but internal divisions and the fear of total collapse pushed Emperor Hirohito to act.

On August 15th, Hirohito addressed the nation by radio. It was the first time the Japanese people had ever heard the emperor's voice. He told them the war must end, stating that continuing to fight would only bring further suffering. For many listeners, the speech was difficult to understand, both because of its formal language and the shock of hearing it at all. Still, the message was clear: Japan would surrender.

The decision to drop the atomic bombs has remained controversial. Some American officials argued it was necessary to force Japan's surrender without a costly invasion of the home islands. Others believed Japan was already on the verge of collapse and that alternatives, such as a demonstration of the bomb's power or modifying surrender terms to preserve the emperor, were not seriously explored. Critics also point to the speed with which the second bomb was used, leaving little time for Japan to respond to Hiroshima.

On the ground, the effects were catastrophic. The blasts in Hiroshima and Nagasaki killed tens of thousands instantly and left many more to suffer from burns, radiation sickness, and long-term illnesses, including cancer and genetic damage. Entire neighborhoods were flattened, and survivors—known as *hibakusha*—faced discrimination for years due to fears of contamination. Environmental effects included contaminated water, soil, and increased rates of birth defects.

After Japan surrendered, it adopted a new constitution, which was largely written under the supervision of American officials. The country was occupied by US forces led by General Douglas MacArthur. Japan was **accused** of committing war crimes that had resulted in the deaths of as many as fourteen million people across Asia.

One of the darkest aspects of Japan's wartime conduct was Unit 731, a covert military program based in **Manchuria** that conducted human experimentation under the guise of medical research. Prisoners, many of them Chinese civilians but also Koreans, Soviets, and others, were subjected to vivisection, biological weapons testing, and forced exposure to extreme conditions without anesthesia. Estimates of those killed range into the thousands.

After the war, the US quietly granted immunity to many of Unit 731's leaders in exchange for access to their research, which was seen as valuable for biological warfare. As a result, few were prosecuted, and public discussion of the unit was suppressed in both Japan and the United States for decades.

Although those involved in Unit 731 largely did not face repercussions, several high-ranking officials were **convicted** and executed, including Prime Minister Hideki Tōjō, former Prime Minister Kōki Hirota, General Kenji Doihara, General Heitarō Kimura, and General Akira Mutō. Emperor Hirohito was spared. Many believe this was because his symbolic role as emperor was crucial to MacArthur's plan for stabilizing Japan. Hirohito played an important part in transforming Japan from a militarist empire into a peaceful nation focused on reconstruction and economic growth.

Hirohito was compelled to publicly declare that he was not a divine being but rather a constitutional monarch representing his people, like other modern monarchs. He continued to perform ceremonial **duties** and appeared to accept his new role as a figurehead of peace. His personal transformation reflected that of his nation, as Japan redirected its energy from conquest to rebuilding, modernization, and prosperity.

Hirohito reigned **until** his death in 1989, providing stability during Japan's long postwar recovery. He met with world leaders, including US President Gerald Ford in 1975. His presence offered a sense of continuity through decades of change. By the end of his life, Japan had become a democratic and prosperous nation. It was far different from the empire he once ruled.

Summary Timeline — The Shōwa Era

- 1901 CE – Birth of Crown Prince Hirohito.
- 1912 CE – Emperor Meiji dies; Emperor Taishō succeeds.
- 1919 CE – Emperor Taishō withdraws from public duties because of illness.
- 1921 CE – Hirohito becomes regent for his ailing father.
- 1923 CE – Great Kantō earthquake and the subsequent Kantō Massacre of ethnic Koreans.
- 1928 CE – Warlord Zhang Zuolin assassinated by Kwantung Army officers in Manchuria.
- 1929 CE – Prime Minister Tanaka Giichi resigns after covering up the assassination.
- 1931 CE – Prime Minister Hamaguchi Osachi dies from wounds from an assassination attempt.
- 1932 CE – Prime Minister Inukai Tsuyoshi assassinated by young naval officers; civilian leadership collapses.
- 1932 CE – Manchukuo established as a puppet state in Manchuria.
- 1935 CE – Lieutenant Colonel Aizawa kills Major General Nagata; extremists hail him as a hero.
- 1936 CE – The February 26 Incident: attempted coup by young army officers; revolt suppressed.
- 1937 CE – Japan launches a full-scale invasion of China, beginning the Second Sino-Japanese War.
- 1940 CE – Japan joins Germany and Italy in the Tripartite Pact; Japan enters World War II.
- 1941 CE – Attack on Pearl Harbor.
- 1942 CE – Early victories across the Pacific; Japanese control extends to Southeast Asia.
- 1944 CE – US forces recapture the Philippines; Japan begins to lose the war.
- 1945 CE – Atomic bombings of Hiroshima and Nagasaki; Emperor Hirohito announces Japan's surrender; end of the war and of the empire's expansion.

- 1975 CE – Emperor Hirohito visits US President Gerald Ford, symbolizing postwar reconciliation.
- 1989 CE – Emperor Hirohito dies; end of the Shōwa era.

Chapter 10: Modern Japan

After the close of World War II, Japan seemed to be a devastated country without a future. However, by the 1960s, it had become the third-largest economy in the world after the United States and the Soviet Union. This period, from the 1950s to the mid-1970s, is often referred to as the "Japanese Miracle." It was a period of rapid change and extreme economic growth that allowed Japan to rise from the ashes of war to become an economic powerhouse.

Japan benefited from the economic boom caused by the Cold War, during which the United States funneled money into Japan to support the Korean War and to maintain a strategic buffer against Soviet influence in Asia. Because of Japan's location, it became an obvious choice to supply the US Armed Forces with the materials and equipment needed to fight in Korea.

The US occupation of Japan ended in 1952, and by then—thanks partly to government reforms and American economic stimulus—the nation was once again a global trading power. Japan's government, specifically the Ministry of International Trade and Industry (MITI), adopted the "Inclined Production Mode," which focused on producing key raw materials such as steel, coal, and cotton. The government also encouraged women to join the workforce, something that had previously been uncommon.

After the US withdrawal, Japan concentrated on heavy industrialization. A system known as "over-loaning," in which companies borrowed beyond their means from city banks that in turn borrowed from the Bank of Japan, allowed the central bank to maintain control over much of the nation's economic growth. The result was the rise of large corporate conglomerates, or *keiretsu*, which thrived under relaxed anti-monopoly laws. Examples of keiretsu include Toyota, Mitsubishi, Kawasaki, Hitotsubashi Group (a major publishing house), and Sega Sammy Holdings.

During this period, Japan saw a dramatic increase in its standard of living as it completed its industrialization process. This era is often called the "Golden Sixties." The decade began with Prime Minister Hayato Ikeda announcing a plan to double Japan's economy within ten years. Ikeda strengthened the US-Japanese alliance and sought to calm the anti-US sentiment that had erupted during the 1960 Anpo protests, which opposed the US right to maintain military bases in Japan.

Ikeda, unlike his predecessor, adopted a stance of tolerance and patience. He held a summit with President John F. Kennedy to assure the United States that Japan would support its Cold War policies, including support for Taiwan's independence and non-recognition of mainland China. Kennedy had even planned to visit Tokyo, but he was assassinated before he could make the trip.

Ikeda's administration expanded Japan's social safety net and established a national pension plan. Tokyo hosted the 1964 Summer Olympics, making up for its earlier selection in 1940, which had been canceled due to Japan's invasion of China and the outbreak of World War II. These were the first Olympics held in Asia and also the debut of the Paralympic Games. They were the first Olympic Games to be telecast via satellite to other parts of the world.

Japan showcased its technological achievements during the Olympics. Toshiba's new color broadcasting system was used to record events such as judo and sumo demonstrations in color, though these broadcasts were limited to domestic audiences. These Olympic Games marked the debut of judo. Japan finished third in the medal count, behind the United States and the Soviet Union. Among the highlights was the undefeated performance of Osamu Watanabe in freestyle wrestling, who retired after winning gold and remains the only wrestler in history to finish his career without a single loss.

Ikeda's administration championed a mixed economic model featuring low interest rates and heavy investment in infrastructure and communications. It also encouraged liberal trade policies, promoting free trade with minimal restrictions on imports and exports. However, many Japanese companies resisted this approach. The media dubbed the liberalization of trade as the "second coming of the Black Ships," referencing Commodore Perry's infamous arrival in Tokyo Bay.

Ikeda served two terms. By the end of his second term, Japan's economy was growing at a remarkable rate of around 13 percent annually. His successor, Eisaku Satō, served the longest consecutive term of that era, from 1964 to 1972. Under his leadership, Japan continued its phenomenal growth. Satō supported the United States during the Vietnam War, which sparked protests at home, but overall, he was a well-liked prime minister, thanks largely to the prosperity Japan enjoyed during his time in office.

Satō, a member of the Liberal Democratic Party (LDP), was openly opposed to the communist government of the People's Republic of China and even opposed US President Nixon's visit to China in 1972. The prime minister was convinced that Japan needed nuclear weapons to safeguard against China, but the United States opposed such measures. Satō ultimately signed the Nuclear Non-Proliferation Treaty in 1970 and was awarded the Nobel Peace Prize in 1974, largely for his role in promoting Japan's "Three Non-Nuclear Principles." These principles stated that Japan would not possess nuclear weapons, not produce them, and not permit their introduction into Japanese territory.

Okinawa (the largest of the Ryukyu Islands) had been in US hands since the end of World War II. However, Satō was able to work out an agreement with President Nixon in which Okinawa would be returned to Japan while allowing the US to maintain military bases on the islands. The official reversion took place in 1972, the same year Satō retired as prime minister.

He was succeeded by Kakuei Tanaka, who had previously worked under Ikeda and Satō in various roles. Tanaka normalized relations with China and met with Chairman Mao Zedong in 1972. His administration expanded welfare programs and invested heavily in infrastructure. However, the country faced an economic downturn during the 1973 oil crisis. Confronted by that crisis and a scandal involving his business dealings, particularly the Lockheed bribery scandal, Tanaka resigned in 1974.

The case involved payments from the Lockheed Corporation to secure the sale of its aircraft to All Nippon Airways. The revelation came from hearings in the United States and quickly drew public outrage in Japan. Tanaka denied the accusations but was later arrested in 1976 and found guilty in 1983. However, even after stepping down, he continued to wield influence within the Liberal Democratic Party.

He was followed by Takeo Miki, who was selected by leaders of the Liberal Democratic Party for his integrity and lack of strong ties to any particular power base. Miki attempted to reform the LDP while in office, especially by trying to stamp out corruption, but he was not entirely successful. This made him **unpopular** within his own party, and he was forced to resign in 1976.

The Japanese economic miracle was over by this point. A series of prime ministers oversaw a period of slowed growth. What endured from this period was not just infrastructure and social welfare but also Japan's enormous influence on global popular culture. This era saw the birth of kaiju monster films—most famously *Godzilla*—as well as the rise of anime, a style of animation that began in the 1960s and **continues** to this day.

Nintendo, a company founded in 1889, first became publicly traded in the 1960s and entered the video game **market** with its Color TV-Game console in 1977. Japanese arcade games became smash hits worldwide, replacing more expensive physical toys after the oil crisis. Nintendo went on to release Donkey Kong in 1981 and Super Mario Bros. in 1985, becoming an industry giant.

Japanese writers like Yasunari Kawabata and Yukio Mishima were active during this period. Kawabata won the 1968 Nobel Prize in Literature. American troops stationed in Japan brought home artifacts, stories, **and** cultural influences that inspired generations of Americans to study Zen Buddhism, create Zen gardens, practice karate, and drink green tea.

In 1989, Emperor Hirohito died at the age of eighty-eight. He was posthumously given the name Emperor Shōwa. His reign lasted sixty-two years, making him one of the longest-reigning monarchs in history. He was succeeded by his son, Akihito, who was fifty-five at the time. Akihito worked tirelessly to express **sorrow** and apologize for the atrocities committed by Japan during World War II. He also sought to connect more directly with the Japanese people by personally visiting every prefecture. Akihito's reign, from 1989 to 2019, is called the Heisei era.

In 1989, Japan's economy had recovered from the oil crisis of the 1970s and entered a period of significant growth. The Tokyo Stock Exchange reached record highs that year, but this was fueled by inflated real estate and stock values, creating what came to be known as the "bubble economy." In 1990, the stock market fell to half its value, and by 1992, the bubble had burst. This began the so-called "Lost Decade," which refers primarily to the 1990s, though economic stagnation continued well into the early 21st century.

In the 1990s, the Japanese economy grew by only about 1 percent annually—an alarming drop from the height of the Japanese economic miracle. This slowdown was partly caused by Japanese banks continuing to over-lend to companies that were unprofitable and financially insecure, often referred to as "zombie firms." As these firms collapsed, they dragged many banks down with them, leading to a wave of consolidation that resulted in four major national banks in Japan.

Japanese companies that had once dominated global markets were now facing serious competition from other Asian economies, especially South Korea and China. Wages stagnated, and many jobs became temporary or part-time positions without benefits.

The Liberal Democratic Party lost support after the 1988 Recruit Scandal, which involved insider trading and political corruption. Shares in Recruit Cosmos, a real estate subsidiary, had been offered to politicians, bureaucrats, and business leaders before the company went public, allowing them to profit illegally. The scandal implicated members of both major parties and eroded confidence in Japan's political system. The LDP briefly lost power in 1993 but returned the following year by helping elect Tomiichi Murayama of the Japan Socialist Party as prime minister through a coalition government.

Public trust was tested again in 1995. In January, the Great Hanshin earthquake struck the city of Kobe and surrounding areas, killing more than six thousand people and leaving hundreds of thousands homeless. The government's slow and disorganized response drew widespread criticism, as many felt the central authorities were unprepared and indifferent to the suffering of victims. Only two months later, Japan was shaken again by the Aum Shinrikyō sarin gas attacks on the Tokyo subway. Members of the religious cult Aum Shinrikyō released nerve gas during the morning rush hour, killing thirteen people and injuring thousands. The attacks exposed serious weaknesses in Japan's emergency response system and raised concerns about the growing alienation and extremism within parts of Japanese society. As a result of these events, non-governmental organizations were established to provide relief and continue to play key roles in disaster response.

It was also during the 1990s that Japan began to take cautious steps toward becoming a more active **military** power. It sent financial aid for the Gulf War in 1991, even though direct participation was restricted by Article 9 of the Japanese Constitution, which prohibits offensive military actions. Later, in 2003, Japan sent about one thousand members of the Japan Self-Defense Forces to Iraq to assist with reconstruction efforts following the Iraq War.

By 2008, Greater Tokyo had become the largest metropolitan economy in the world and the most populous metropolitan area. In 2010, Japan's population peaked at around 128 million, but it has been in **decline** since due to a persistently low birth rate. In 2011, Japan was struck by the strongest earthquake ever recorded in the country—a magnitude 9.0 quake known as the Great East Japan earthquake or the Tōhoku earthquake. This disaster triggered the Fukushima Daiichi Nuclear Disaster, the worst nuclear accident since Chernobyl in 1986.

Japan's economy did not begin to see substantial recovery until around 2018, due in large part to the **policies** of Prime Minister Shinzō Abe, a member of the LDP. His economic program, often called "Abenomics," sought to revive growth after two decades of stagnation through a combination of aggressive monetary easing, increased government spending, and structural reforms. Abe worked closely with the Bank of Japan to combat deflation by expanding the money supply and keeping interest rates near zero. His government also encouraged corporate investment, greater participation of women in the workforce, and limited immigration to address labor shortages.

Emperor Akihito abdicated in 2019, citing declining health. He was succeeded by his son, Emperor Naruhito, marking the beginning of the Reiwa era. In 2020, Shinzō Abe became the longest-serving prime minister in Japanese history. As of this writing, every prime minister has been a member of the LDP since then.

In 2021, due to the pandemic, the postponed Summer Olympics were finally held in Tokyo. In 2022, after resigning as prime minister, Shinzō Abe was assassinated while giving a campaign speech in Nara. The killer, who used an improvised firearm, claimed to have acted out of resentment toward the Unification Church (often called the

"Moonies"). He said he targeted Abe because of the former prime minister's connection to the organization.

The Unification Church was founded in South Korea in 1954 by Sun Myung Moon, a self-proclaimed messiah who taught a unique interpretation of Christianity focused on spiritual "purification" and global unity. The church spread rapidly during the Cold War and established strong ties with conservative political movements in Japan, South Korea, and the United States. In Japan, it gained influence through its staunch anti-communist stance and close association with right-leaning groups within the Liberal Democratic Party.

However, the church also became notorious for its aggressive fundraising and recruitment practices. Many followers were persuaded to make enormous financial donations, often leading to bankruptcy or family hardship. Over the decades, thousands of Japanese families filed complaints claiming they had been exploited. The church was accused of using guilt-based persuasion, telling followers their ancestors' souls could only be saved by giving large monetary offerings.

After Abe's assassination, the revelation that numerous LDP politicians, including Abe himself, had accepted support or appeared at church-related events sparked outrage. It was not illegal to associate with the church, but many Japanese saw these connections as ethically troubling, given the group's history of exploiting vulnerable people. For the public, the scandal symbolized the blurred line between religion and politics in Japan and raised uncomfortable questions about how fringe organizations could influence national leaders.

Summary Timeline – Modern Japan

- 1988 CE – The Liberal Democratic Party loses support after the Recruit Scandal involving insider trading and corruption.
- 1994 CE – The LDP helps elect Socialist Prime Minister Tomiichi Murayama through a coalition government.
- 1995 CE – The Great Hanshin earthquake and Aum Shinrikyō sarin-gas attacks shake public confidence in the government.
- 2003 CE – About one thousand Self-Defense Force personnel are sent to Iraq for reconstruction assistance.
- 2008 CE – Greater Tokyo becomes the world's largest city economy.
- 2010 CE – Japan's population peaks at roughly 128 million.

- 2011 CE – The Great East Japan earthquake and Fukushima nuclear disaster devastate northeastern Japan.
- 2018 CE – Economic recovery begins under the policies of Prime Minister Shinzō Abe.
- 2019 CE – Emperor Akihito abdicates; Emperor Naruhito ascends, beginning the Reiwa era.
- 2020 CE – Shinzō Abe becomes Japan's longest-serving prime minister.
- 2021 CE – Tokyo hosts the Summer Olympics amid the pandemic.
- 2022 CE – Former Prime Minister Shinzō Abe is assassinated while campaigning.

Conclusion

Japan continues to be a place of extremes. As a nation, it has struggled with a past that is at times glorious and at others unsettling. Yet, it stands at the edge of the future, ready to embrace and create new technologies that improve and expand human understanding. Scientists from Japan regularly win international awards and contribute to global research, while archaeologists and historians continue to uncover new insights into Japan's ancient past.

Japan still holds an air of mystery for much of the Western world, even as its cultural influence is impossible to ignore. Two of the most successful intellectual properties of all time—Pokémon and Hello Kitty—are Japanese. Japan's art, design, cuisine, and technology shape global trends. Its film, literature, and animation have inspired generations.

Politically, Japan today is a stable democracy with one of the highest standards of living in the world. The country continues to grapple with a declining population and a rapidly aging society—challenges that have reshaped its economy, workforce, and family life. Despite these difficulties, Japan is the world's third-largest economy and a leader in robotics, renewable energy, and high-speed transportation. Tokyo stands as one of the most advanced cities on Earth, blending ancient shrines with neon skylines and cutting-edge technology.

Yet, this economic strength faces an unexpected challenge from its overwhelming success. Japan welcomed a record 36.9 million foreign visitors in 2024, shattering the previous high of 31.9 million set before the pandemic. The surge has continued into 2025, with visitor numbers climbing steadily month after month. What was once seen as a triumph has become a double-edged sword. Tourism spending now ranks as Japan's second-largest export industry after automobiles, pumping billions into the economy, yet the sheer weight of these numbers is transforming beloved neighborhoods and sacred sites in ways no one anticipated.

Walk through Kyoto's ancient Gion district today, and you'll find something has changed. Local residents speak of feeling like strangers in their own city, pushed to the margins by selfie-seeking crowds. The harassment of geisha and maiko (apprentice geisha) became so severe that authorities banned tourists entirely from certain backstreets. In Fujikawaguchiko, a convenience store gained such viral fame for its view of Mount Fuji that the town erected a large black screen to block the sight. They saw it as the only way to restore peace to a neighborhood overrun by photographers. These aren't isolated incidents. They're symptoms of what the Japanese call *kankō kōgai*—tourism pollution.

The Japanese government finds itself in a delicate position, celebrating record numbers while scrambling to address their consequences. Officials have allocated billions of yen to combat overtourism, funding everything from crowd-monitoring systems to initiatives that steer visitors toward less-traveled regions. Some attractions have introduced tiered pricing, with international visitors paying more than locals. Another issue is that 73 percent of overnight stays are in just five prefectures, leaving much of Japan's beauty largely undiscovered.

Japanese people view this tourism boom differently. The weak yen has made Japan remarkably affordable for foreign visitors, yet this same currency weakness makes it harder for Japanese citizens to travel abroad themselves. The money flowing in helps businesses and creates jobs, but residents in Kyoto, Tokyo, and Osaka increasingly find themselves priced out of their own neighborhoods, stuck in traffic jams of tour buses, and unable to get seats on trains they've ridden their entire lives.

The government has set an ambitious target of sixty million visitors by 2030. Whether Japan can achieve this goal while preserving what makes it special remains one of the country's most pressing questions. The very qualities that draw people to Japan—the tranquility of its temples, the orderliness of its streets, and the careful preservation of tradition—are the same qualities most threatened by their arrival.

Another threat Japan faces today is not foreign conflict but the changing climate itself. Its geographical position makes it particularly vulnerable to rising temperatures, heavier rainfall, and more frequent typhoons. These changes have affected harvests, coral reefs, and coastal communities. Japan has taken a leading role in addressing climate change and developing sustainable technologies.

The Japanese Self-Defense Forces remain among the most capable in the world, though it is constitutionally bound to act only in defense. In recent years, there have been debates about revising Article 9 of the Constitution to allow for a more active military role as global tensions rise. Yet, Japan continues to advocate for diplomacy and peace, often leading humanitarian and disaster relief efforts across Asia.

If Japanese history teaches us anything, it is never to underestimate the Japanese people. They are guided as much by intellect and innovation as by an enduring and indomitable spirit. From rebuilding after wars to thriving amidst adversity, Japan has shown the world that resilience, discipline, and imagination can turn even the harshest trials into opportunities for renewal.

In many ways, Japan embodies both the memory of its past and the promise of the future. It is a nation forever looking forward while never forgetting where it has come from.

Here's another book by Enthralling History that you might like

Free limited time bonus

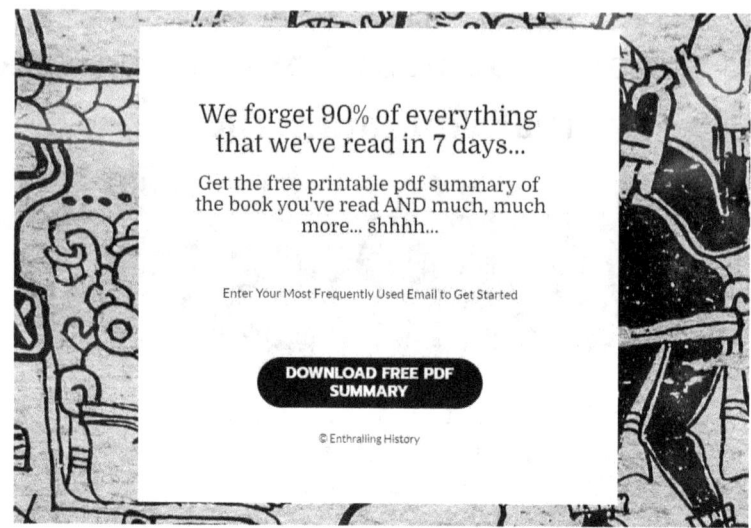

Stop for a moment. We have a free bonus set up for you. The problem is this: we forget 90% of everything that we read after 7 days. Crazy fact, right? Here's the solution: we've created a printable, 1-page pdf summary for this book that you're reading now. All you have to do to get your free pdf summary is to go to the following website:
https://livetolearn.lpages.co/enthrallinghistory/

Or, Scan the QR code!

Once you do, it will be intuitive. Enjoy, and thank you!

Works Cited

奈良文化財研究所ホームページ, https://www.nabunken.go.jp/. Accessed 25 August 2024.

Japanese Wiki Corpus, https://www.japanesewiki.com/. Accessed 25 August 2024.

4-7 The 2.26 Incident of 1936 | Modern Japan in archives, https://www.ndl.go.jp/modern/e/cha4/description07.html. Accessed 6 November 2024.

Benedict, Ruth. *The Chrysanthemum and the Sword: Patterns of Japanese Culture*. Houghton Mifflin, 2005.

Brown, Delmer M. "The Impact of Firearms on Japanese Warfare." *The Far Eastern Quarterly*, vol. 7, no. 3, 1948, pp. 236-53. *jstor*, https://doi.org/10.2307/2048846. Accessed 9 Oct 2024.

"Chapter Two." *A Bowl for a Coin: A Commodity History of Japanese Tea*, by William Wayne Farris, Knowledge Unlatched, 2019. Accessed 16 August 2024.

Clements, Jonathan. *A Brief History of Japan: Samurai, Shogun and Zen: The Extraordinary Story of the Land of the Rising Sun*. Tuttle Publishing, 2017.

Curry, Andrew. "Turning Japanese." *Archaeology*, vol. 61, no. 1, 2008, pp. 18-65. *jstor.org*, http://www.jstor.org/stable/41780320. Accessed 23 June 2024.

Duus, Peter, et al., editors. *The Japanese Wartime Empire, 1931-1945*. Princeton University Press, 1996.

"Emperor Hirohito and PM Yoshida | American Experience." *PBS*, https://www.pbs.org/wgbh/americanexperience/features/macarthur-emperor-hirohito-and-pm-yoshida/. Accessed 2 November 2024.

Farris, William W. "Trade, Money, and Merchants in Nara Japan." *Monumenta Nipponica*, vol. 53, no. 3, 1998, pp. 303-34. *jstor*, https://doi.org/10.2307/2385718. Accessed 9 July 2024.

"History of Zen Buddhism | International Zen Association." *Association Zen Internationale*, https://www.zen-azi.org/en/history-zen-buddhism. Accessed 13 August 2024.

"History - Tokugawa Ieyasu." *BBC*, https://www.bbc.co.uk/history/historic_figures/ieyasu_tokugawa.shtml. Accessed 16 October 2024.

Ishii, Mikiko. "The Noh Theater: Mirror, Mask, and Madness." *Comparative Drama*, vol. 28, no. 1, 1994, pp. 43-66. *jstor*. Accessed 20 Sept 2024.

Kazui, Tashiro, and Susan Downing Videen. "Foreign Relations during the Edo Period: Sakoku Reexamined." *Journal of Japanese Studies*, vol. 8, no. 2, 1982, pp. 283-306. *jstor*. Accessed 17 Oct 2024.

Pearson, Richard. "Debating Jomon Social Complexity." *Asian Perspectives*, vol. 46, no. 2, 2007, pp. 361-88. *JSTOR*, http://www.jstor.org/stable/42928722. Accessed 24 June 2024.

Spafford, David. "Emperor and Shogun, Pope and King: The Development of Japan's Warrior Aristocracy." *Bulletin of the Detroit Institute of Arts*, vol. 88, no. 1/4, 2014, pp. 10-19. *jstor*, http://www.jstor.org/stable/43493624. Accessed 12 July 2024.

Suzuki, Daisetz Teitaro. *Introduction to Zen Buddhism, Including a Manual of Zen Buddhism*. Causeway Books, 1974.

Takashi, Kato. "Edo in the Seventeenth Century: Aspects of Urban Development in a Segregated Society." *Urban History*, vol. 27, no. 2, 2000, pp. 189-210. *jstor*. Accessed 17 Oct 2024.

Turnbull, Stephen. "The Onin War: A Turning Point in Samurai History." *Medieval Warfare*, vol. 10, no. 2, 2020, pp. 38-45. *jstor*, https://www.jstor.org/stable/48683814. Accessed 29 09 2024.

Walker, Brett L. *A Concise History of Japan*. Cambridge University Press, 2015.

Yoshie, Akiko. "Gendered Interpretations of Female Rule: The Case of Himiko, Ruler of Yamatai." *U.S. -Japan Women's Journal*, vol. 44, no. 1, 2013, pp. 3-23. *JSTOR*, http://www.jstor.org/stable/42771843. Accessed 29 June 2024.

Image Sources

1. https://commons.wikimedia.org/wiki/File:Sasaki_Toyokichi_-_Nihon_hana_zue_-_Walters_95208.jpg
2. Original: Ash Crow and Maximilian Dörrbecker (Chumwa) Vector: AntiCompositeNumber, CC BY-SA 3.0 <https://creativecommons.org/licenses/by-sa/3.0>, via Wikimedia Commons, https://commons.wikimedia.org/wiki/File:Gempei_war-battles.svg
3. https://commons.wikimedia.org/wiki/File:Emperor_Go-Daigo.jpg
4. https://commons.wikimedia.org/wiki/File:Ashikaga_Takauji.JPG
5. https://commons.wikimedia.org/wiki/File:Sengoku_period_battle.jpg
6. https://commons.wikimedia.org/wiki/File:Odanobunaga.jpg
7. https://commons.wikimedia.org/wiki/File:Tokugawa_Ieyasu2.JPG
8. https://commons.wikimedia.org/wiki/File:Meiji_Emperor_painted_by_Takagi_Haisui.jpg
9. https://commons.wikimedia.org/wiki/File:Emperor_Sh%C5%8Dwa_official_portrait_1_(cropped).jpg
10. Kokiri at English Wikipedia, modifications by Huhsunqu and Markalexander100., CC BY-SA 3.0 <http://creativecommons.org/licenses/by-sa/3.0/>, via Wikimedia Commons, https://commons.wikimedia.org/wiki/File:Japanese_Empire2.png

www.ingramcontent.com/pod-product-compliance
Lightning Source LLC
Chambersburg PA
CBHW050335010526
44119CB00004B/150